# How To
# FLY FISH
# ALASKA

# Jim Repine

FRANK AMATO
PUBLICATIONS

# ── Dedication ──

## To Jubal, My Best Friend

**Cover Photo by Marty Sherman**            **Flies tied by Randy Stetzer**

Fish drawings by Ron Pittard. For complete color game fish species wall posters
contact: Windsor Publications, 2515 Windsor Circle, Eugene, OR 97405

ISBN 0-936608-68-4 • Copyright 1988 • Jim Repine
Typesetting: Chris Mazzuca • Book Design: Joyce Herbst
Printed in U.S.A.

# Contents

# Jim Repine's Alaska Fishing Map

For a comprehensive fishing map of Alaska order a copy of *Jim Repine's Alaska Fishing Map.* It measures 44 inches by 33 inches (two sheets printed both sides) and is in two colors. Hundreds of the best rivers, lakes and salt water fishing areas are shown and special emphasis is placed on 74 of the very best rivers, lakes and saltwater fishing areas including complete listings of the gamefish species available. Also included are knot illustrations and month by month explanations of the best fishing. Tourist addresses and bibliography of other fishing books included. A five thousand word article explains tackle needed as well as fly-out and drive-to information.

Here is what one reviewer has said: "When I say this one has drawn rave reviews, believe me. The two-sided color production, without any question on my part, is the most complete and informative package ever offered to the general public on Alaska. Nobody going to Alaska should leave the Lower 48 without purchasing this map that tells you everything from where to fish, how to dress, float trips, canoeing, knot-tying, well, it's all there and more. I think so much of the Repine-Amato offering I'd need to be life-threatened before allowing my copy outside our house."          *Bud Leavitt, Bangor Daily News, Maine.*

Avialable from Frank Amato Publications, Box 02112, Portland, Oregon 97202. (503) 653-8108     $8.95 Postpaid.

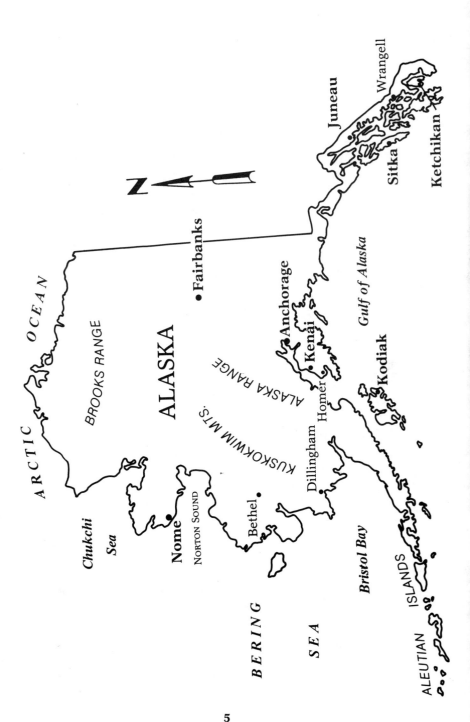

ARCTIC OCEAN

BROOKS RANGE

ALASKA

•Fairbanks

N

Chukchi Sea

Nome
NORTON SOUND

Bethel •

KUSKOKWIM MTS.

ALASKA RANGE

Anchorage
•Kenai
Homer

Gulf of Alaska

Kodiak

Dillingham •

BERING SEA

Bristol Bay

ALEUTIAN ISLANDS

Juneau

Wrangell

Sitka

Ketchikan

5

# Foreword

J im Repine writes with depth and understanding of the fly fishing in Alaska, his adopted home. For him it has proven to be an angler's heaven and he fills his life there with fly fishing's rich rewards. When I go to Alaska again this year, Jim will be beside me in the essence of his thoughts and memories because of this book which tells me things about him that fishing with him a few years back did not.

Although the most eager anglers will probably seek the 10- to 20-lb. rainbows that often require a fly near the bottom which Jim covers, he also writes of the two- to three-pounders that tend to get scant notice in Alaskan fishing stories. These are the fish that remind me of my long-ago wonderful days in New York and California when there were lots of wild trout of that size and only a few of us fly fishermen to share them. Those were great times in my memory and development as an angler and with a helping hand from Jim and Alaska they are still around for fly fishermen to enjoy.

Repine covers all the fly-catchable species, in detail, from the great king salmon to the grayling and pike and gives the key to some of the secret places he has treasured. As a writer he has had opportunities to fish at the most celebrated lodges and the most famous of the fishing waters. More than that, he has fished the easier to reach, less dramatic, more available places where the cost is low but where there are great angling memories to be made.

This book will tell you where to find your kind of fly fishing in angling's last and greatest treasure trove. You'll fish Alaska with some basic understanding and I hope that when you do some of Jim's love of that wild and wonderful country will touch you, too.

*Lee Wulff*

# ─── Introduction ───

No one knows when the first feathered hook was cast in Alaska but it likely goes back farther than most of us think. Native artifacts, hundreds of years old, reveal some use of feathers attached to a hook as a jigging lure but it was hand-tossed or lowered through the ice. The purest original pattern created here so far, or so the story goes, was an attempted copy of an ivory jigging lure fished under the ice near Kotzebue by an Eskimo woman named Mary Ann. It's a beautiful thing, ivory floss, silver tinsel striped body and wing, jungle cock eyes and a red tail. But who first used a long rod to angle with a fly here has long been forgotten.

Lee Wulff, born in Valdez, Alaska, over eighty years ago, had his first fly fishing instruction from the town jailer, an English ex-patriot, but doesn't recall now how long the man had been there. And I can't yet find anything written indicating early Russian angling. It seems likely then that Alaska's remarkable collection of trout, char, grayling, pike, sheefish and salmon have known our kind, if only a handful, for at least a century. But for however slight the impact had been until a decade ago, it is all quickly changing now. A full scale explosion of participation is annually mushrooming the number of anglers here, visitors and residents, until the opportunity to find that pristine situation, miles of gorgeous streams, lots of fish of amazing size, with no one else around, has nearly disappeared. But not altogether.

Five-hundred eighty-six thousand (586,000) square miles, if you can imagine it, with millions of lakes, thousands of miles of streams coursing through some of the most remote country left on Earth, still has secret hide-aways but discovering them is no longer easy. Alaska has become like the rest of the western United States with nearly all of its most prolific and desirable water long since discovered and in most cases already serviced by one to several commercial operators. But whatever this fishery lacks for the solitude seeker it still more than makes up for in breathtaking scenery, a cornucopia of species and a growing number of first class facilities. The trade, if you will, has been aesthetics for comfort and ease of access, but frankly, now that I'm on the far side of 50, it doesn't seem quite the tragedy I'd always been so terrified of.

The most important contribution fly fishing has made to Alaska, as elsewhere, has been the introduction and promotion of angling ethics, particularly from the aspect of conservation. Low kill, catch and release philosophies acceptable among visiting anglers enabled the early lodge operators to establish conservative standards. In fact today, you can pretty much judge the quality of individual Alaskan lodges by their kill policies. There are few other examples, worldwide, offering more dramatic proof that the time to protect a fishery is while it is still at a first class level.

But just as surely as increased pressure has forced some unpleasant changes, the steady influx of new people is also bringing a maturing to Alaska's fly fishing community. There are clubs around now making serious efforts to educate any one interested in taking up the sport. Tying seminars, casting instruction and information swapping is taking hold. Enough so that beginners don't have to look so far anymore for help and Anchorage at least even offers a choice of good shops.

I go back to the late '60s here and it has been the best two decades of my life, by far. So what this book will try to do is share as much as I can recall of those wonderful years in hopes that something within these pages might be of help to you.

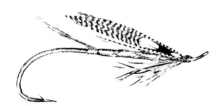

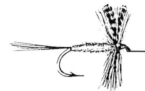

# Chapter 1

# Why the Fly

**W**hen I arrived in Alaska in the late '60s fly fishing wasn't exactly the rage. Of course the few lodges then operating attracted a fair percentage of long rod fanciers and a handful of locals were quietly having a ball but the "sportfishing" scene was all part of summer-long efforts to fill freezers with enough corpses of wild creatures to feed a family of ten through the long cold winter. Whether one actually had a family didn't seem to matter. Not even $100,000 plus per annum doctors and lawyers were excused. If you were an adult, white male your obligation to frontier masculinity demanded that you butcher enough each season to last ten people for about eight months.

What it really was (a lot of it still continues) was

blood greed in the land of plenty. For example, I saw a party of four meet the float plane that came to pick them up at the end of a three-day float trip. Each "sportsman" had a cooler filled with his legal possession of 20 rainbow trout. None were under 20 inches as these egg fishermen had "thrown" the little ones back. Everyone laughed when the pilot dumped the first two cooler loads in the river. It seems there was a half a case of beer they had failed to finish and wanted to take home. The fish would put them overweight. It was typical, the prevailing attitude.

I sat in the kitchen of an Anchorage orthodonist one afternoon. The home was lovely, worth $300,000, conservatively. He wanted to go fishing but only if he was sure to bring back limits of fish. Through the window we could see Canadian geese he'd killed a few days before, on the ground in the backyard, rotting.

I was roundly cursed once on the Kenai River for releasing a salmon. And the most common answer, in those days, from late August through November, to "How are you?", "How's it going?", even "Long time no see" or "Good morning" was, "Get your moose yet?"

Maybe the epitome of it all is the Russian River. An especially beautiful tributary of the Kenai where in 1927, Wulff released dozens of huge rainbow trout in a day. The river was declared "fly fishing only" in 1966. The big attraction is a massive sockeye run. "Sportsmen" turned out in droves, equipped with spinning rods, lead sinkers and streamer flies. Thousands of people each season still crowd the river, "fly fishing" by this method. It's an angler's nightmare.

I'm not an across-the-board, no-kill advocate. I believe though, it's important to set aside some high quality water for catch and release in order for everyone to be able to experience prolific fishing on occasion and have an opportunity, while so doing, to see what it feels like to enjoy the pursuit without the kill. But no one could love frying a pan full of freshly caught trout more than me. The sport's highest moment for me, in fact, is a backpack camp in a wilderness setting, cooking fish I caught for dinner.

What I despise though is callous, cruel, disrespect displayed toward a fellow creature. Sometime, if you've never done this, hold a fish you've landed in your hands. Be very gentle, keep the fish in the water and consider every aspect of this wondrous being. Examine its design. Let yourself be fascinated with the marvel of its coloration. Ponder over its life style. Think of all the rejuvenating, soul-mending adventures fish offer. But mostly, feel the sensually pulsing energy of life force, let your own flow back and never again believe that taking another's life is of little consequence.

The reasons some of us have strong preferences for doing our fishing with fly rods and feathered hooks are probably as varied as the myriad fly patterns created and developed over the past century or two. But we remain a small minority of the sportfishing world. Why?

Some say the skills are too difficult for the masses but I've seen compelling evidence to the contrary. I've watched skilled angling instructors, Mel Krieger for example, transform outright spastics into reasonable casters, good enough to consistently catch fish and enjoy the process, in two-day seminars. I've guided folks who had never had a lesson, read a book or watched a videotape and still managed to cast effectively if not beautifully. But the real proof for me, that anyone can do it, is that I can. Enough said.

Others contend bait, spinning and level wind fishing are so often more productive that most people don't want to change. It's a hard point to argue, partly

*Brooks River Falls sockeye.*

because there are times when it's true. But it goes deeper than that, getting into just what individuals are really seeking when they head for the water.

And the other often-heard opinion is that we're too snobbish, elitist if you will, to attract the common man. Balderdash! I'm as plain as corncob pipes and coonhounds and despise snobbery but I'd rather catch a catfish on a streamer than chicken guts. I do believe though that most people who are going to angle with a fly are already doing it and if it was the only fishing method allowed, 90 percent of the crowds we now find on the streams would return to their bowling alleys and baseball games. In other words, I don't think universal exposure will bring mass defection from the other methods anymore than music classes have lured any real number of rock and rollers to Mozart. It's a matter of taste.

I'm not sure I can identify, much less describe, the basis of even my own fascination for long rods and flies but I vividly recall its birth. I thought about it not long ago. I was standing beside a clear, deep pool on the Talachulitna River. It was about 80 feet across, just below a fast, narrow shoot, an obvious feeding station. There had to be at least one fat rainbow trout lurking there, sucking in whatever tasty morsels the current presented. Jubal stood beside me.

Jubal is an 11-year-old Rhodesian Ridgeback that some people think is my pet. Of course he's not that at all. He's my roommate, best pal and most constant fishing companion. You may or may now know that Ridgebacks come from Africa where they've been touted for years as lion hounds, their hunting pro-wess, legend. But Jubal, after all these years with me, has been perverted, genetic traits from generations of careful breeding, twisted from blood lustful fascina-tion with furry critters to an absolute mania for fish.

His attention was as intently fixed as mine on the size 16 Black Gnat I'd just cast to the head of the pool. It floated high, drifting along with the current.

As we stared, the tiny fly suddenly changed. It wasn't a Black Gnat anymore. I blinked and looked again. It wasn't even an artificial fly. It was a real live mayfly. Impossible, I thought.

I looked down at Jubal. He wasn't there. In his place was another dog, smaller and scruffier. He looked up. I couldn't believe it. It was Ching, my very first dog. But wait a minute! I was eight years old when we got Ching and this is 45 years later.

"What the hell is this?" I mumbled.

Ching, half Chow, half infinite mixture, quickly looked back toward the water. I looked up, astounded to realize I was no longer on a river in Alaska. Why had I thought so? This is Lakeside, Virginia, right? And this is the creek just below the dam. Well, ah, sure it is. I mean of course it is. Why wouldn't it be?

At ten, I had three great loves: fishing, my dog Ching and Juanita Lacey. Since Juanita sat two rows over from me at school, not seeming to know I existed, the first two affections received all my time.

Where only a moment ago, giant cottonwoods stood resplendent in golden September foliage now there were only small swamp oaks. My 80-ft. pool was more like 15 feet across. The water flowed slowly and dark though not unclear. Ching and I stood transfixed as the fly moved along just two or three feet from the bank.

Then it happened. Something (perhaps the only thing) more graphically fascinating than my first glimpse of an unclothed lady. An incident visually burned more deeply into my memory than any other. I still can't describe the excitement.

From some deep, secret hole, Ching and I saw the

15

biggest, darkest old bream either of us had ever imagined slowly rise to the surface beneath the fragile insect. Silently the giant two-pounder, ever so gently, took the fly and vanished. An illusion? Once fly and fish were gone it was as though it never happened except that a remarkable awakening took place in a 10-year-old boy.

I was barely aware of fly fishing. I'd overheard bits and snatches of conversations from older anglers and had pondered over artificial flies on display at the hardware store but I was only schooled in the pole and worm system. I hadn't yet grasped what you did with little hooks with imitation bugs tied around them.

"If I tied one of those artificials on a line, floated it along the same path as that mayfly? Wow!" Life-changing revelation flashed. Ching whimpered. He was looking up the creek.

Another mayfly was floating toward our pool. The same drama unfolded as the fly came beside us. The same dark object became a fish as it neared the surface. Then everything exploded.

I stared in wild-eyed disbelief as a 25-in., 6-lb. rainbow shot into the air for four consecutive leaps before doing a 30-yd. speed trial downriver. Somehow (the reaction of years?), I remained composed enough to retrieve the slack and keep a bend in the rod. Jubal began to bark.

It was a typical September Talachulitna rainbow trout, fat from a summer of ceaseless gorging on salmon eggs, vividly arrayed in exotic tones of silver, white, black and rose-red unique to the trout of the "Tal." My best dry fly catch of a three-day trip, I was tempted to kiss the beauty as I gently held it until it revived enough to be safely released.

God, I thought, kneeling down beside my dog and

looking around at the enchanting scene, what do you suppose Heaven's like to make it nicer than this? The sky was blue, nearly cloudless, the sun, low enough to cast lovely long shadows. The air was crisp, clear and delightful. Sunlight backlit the cottonwood leaves. They glowed.

As Jubal and I watched, a lonely gust of wind moved through the trees. We both thought we heard something. A woman's voice, strangely familiar, calling from some far distance.

"Jimmeee! Jimmy Repine. . .Supper."

The breeze dislodged a large yellow leaf. It fluttered slowly, very slowly, to the Earth.

That's the when but the why remains a mystery especially if you consider that I'm no bug lover. Even growing up in the insect-rich environs of Virginia and Florida, not only tolerant of the crawlers and buzzers then but fascinated with watching and catching june bugs, lightning bugs, ladybugs and granddaddy long legs, most insects now cause me to itch a little. So what is this thing I have about angling with flies?

It may be, in part anyway, the same thrill I once felt fooling an old tom turkey with a call. Twice I killed flushed birds and it had its electricity but after a year listening in the woods and to a record, practicing at home until my long-suffering mother was ready to take a shot at me, I finally got to see a real live turkey, called within gun range. It didn't matter that in the excitement I killed a pine sapling instead of the bird. After that, I could never have felt right again shooting one of those magnificent birds under any other circumstances. Shotgunning rabbits not being hounded by a couple of loudly bawling beagles became less than a sporting thing for me. And before rods and feathers finally displaced my guns altogether, a duck

*Jim and Jubal with a rainbow.*

not lured into decoys by calling ceased to be fair game.

There's a naturalness in presenting something realistic to the fish. When I drift a well-dressed replica of a living insect along the same course real bugs are floating and fool a trout into coming out of its sanctuary, I feel somehow more attuned to, less intrusive of, an addictively attractive environment.

I also have to confess a certain prediliction with trickery. If I can fool you with a card trick or riddle, I like it. I don't want to embarrass you but if I can trick you, harmlessly, there's a joy in it. Maybe there's a similar sense of trickery with an artificial fly? Maybe, but that hardly explains where the magic in plugs and spinners has gone.

I recall the first big (three-pounder) bass I caught. My dad had gotten me a Sears Roebuck complete casting outfit that couldn't have cost more than five bucks. I immediately corrupted the concept by laboriously learning to cast a fly with it, at least 20 feet. In fact, I caught a fair number of the less clever bream from Lakeside Lake that way. And when I discovered my first sponge spider with rubber legs, I started working on the smarter ones including one small bass taken from under a log in the creek. But as remarkable a catch as it seemed, it wasn't one of the monsters I heard older fishermen claim to have taken from the lake. But those guys were pluggers.

It was probably after overheard bragging at the hardware store that I finally determined to devote an entire afternoon away from my sure-fire bream techniques and cast a Jitterbug for as long as it took. Now understand (or remember), ten-year-olds aren't generally known for their attention spans, especially not when casting a lure that feels as big as a hardball. But the third try produced a splashy strike, the splashiest I'd yet encountered. This was no bream or bream-size bass. Good Lord! There were monsters out there.

I'd hardly stopped shaking a half an hour later when it happened again only this time two of the possible six hooks stuck fast and I suddenly had a fish on not only larger than I'd ever handled, it took a classic largemouth jump. You know the one. It seems to take forever, like slow motion, rising out of the water, shaking its head like a bulldog. I still get a rush recalling it.

My first tarpon could have taken a small school of fish that size in a gulp and at 40 pounds was a miracle of explosive energy, though no more exciting. But it wasn't fly fishing that gave me either of those wonderful moments. I hooked the tarpon spinning with a bucktail.

For fly anglers to claim an elevated level of sportsmanship is, at best, arrogant. Yet, during my years guiding, I would have been blind not to have noted the persistent difference in attitudes between fly fishers and others. With few exceptions, if the clients showed up with spinning gear I knew there would be a problem about catch and release or minimal kill, while it rarely even came up with fly anglers. Draw your own conclusions. And I can offer no reasons why a single, barbless hook is any less sporting attached to a spinner or lure. But of all the angling method converts I've come across, and I'm one, I don't remember any one who spent enough time fly fishing to develop any level of skill, then later went back to their old method.

For some folks just casting with a flyrod becomes a pleasure all its own. Again, I can't give a convincing rationale why. But try it, properly instructed, for long enough to get the feel and you may discover you prefer fly fishing on the basis of casting alone. I've stood for hours at fishing shows and watched in awe as master caster, Stan Fagerstrom, casted a level wind bait casting rig. The man's a magician and anything done that well has to be satisfying but it is not as much fun for me as the long rods. A few years back Dave Duncan, the float trip guide, got me interested in drift rod fishing, casting a level wind reel attached to a flyrod length casting rod. Not only is it fun, a lot of fun, it's deadly for fishing larger, fast water rivers. And while it seems a wedding of two great worlds, somehow it's not the same. After several productive outings I find my drift rigs relegated to the same position as my guns. I'm not ready to throw either away and I'm not sure I'll never use them again but when I head for the outdoors, it's Jubal and my flyrod I can't leave behind.

Then there are genetics, the predator instinct in this case. I know it's real in me, in heavy doses and has been as long as I can remember. I did, after all, chase all those bugs as mentioned. I couldn't help it, until I was old enough for bigger things. I'm talking about a boy who at 11 years old, passionately loved sports but traded football shoulder pads he got for Christmas, two days later, for a vintage, single shot, 16 gauge. The first time I sat quietly under a hickory, the ground around me littered with nut cuttings and held my breath while a gray squirrel made its way through the tree tops toward me was incredible. You could hear him for the longest time before he came into sight, all the while knowing the slightest sound or movement would spook him. But I still wish he'd died a little quicker. I never got used to that part.

There were rabbits and birds after that with sightings of deer but at 16 I heard a lovely little three-legged, converted foxhound named Lady, run a raccoon through a pitch dark swamp. It was the siren call of calls for me. Predator juices I'd never known gushed forth. My father was a classical violinist. Doubtless it is from him I acquired a life-long love of music. I played for money at 14, spent my four military years in a Marine Corps band and studied composition in college but not even Mozart stirs me as deeply as the songs of trailing hounds. It consumed me then as its memories occasionally do now. Fishing remained important but until I headed for Alaska in the late '60s, coon hunting was my passion.

Maybe the strangest thing of all, is it was then I discovered catch and release. It dawned on me one night as I was about to kill another of so many coons. He was just sitting on a limb, an easy target, eyes glowing brightly in the flashlight beam. What could it add to kill the very source of our remarkable night's pleasure? Coon skins never brought much, the meat at best, only tolerable, I lowered the rifle and never killed another raccoon. And all that did was make it more fun.

In any event the addiction some of us have for pursuing wild things is obviously natural even though two hundred million others in the U.S. alone don't wish to join us. The million or so of us who continue indulging our chase instincts by angling with a fly though can arguably claim therapeutic merit in our actions. We've only begun, after all, to understand the negative results of repressed instincts. And to those who continue trying to make catch and release somehow an evil perversion because without the kill it's unnatural, just tormenting a fellow creature for depraved pleasure, I offer two thoughts.

Isn't it equally true the only natural reason for making love is to impregnate the female in order to propagate the species? It only feels like that, in Nature's scheme, so we'll get on with it, right? So unless we intend to make a baby — etc., etc. Frankly, even at my age, I'm not ready to go down that path. Now if that don't work for you, how about asking the catchee? At the point of each kill or release, given the vote, how many fish do you think will opt for being bonked?

So maybe it comes down to this. If what you're looking for is another outlet for your competitive drive, something to get you up and going, keeping the old ego stroked (outwitting a creature with a brain the size of a pea), let me urge you to try bowling or racquetball, you're probably already jogging. No, you say? Fishing is what you want? Then go south, young man, and try your hand at bassin' for bucks. Fly fishing would have little meaning for you and I don't want to get stuck for a week in some remote lodge with you.

But if on occasion you feel the need or maybe just the urge to escape the stultifying, destructive, aspects of life and seek a method to repair some of the damage, the unique offerings of angling with a fly might be just right. If you find solace and restoration in the lovely environs of rivers, lakes and streams, fly fishing will require you to spend regular time there. If you enjoy the kindred feeling of involvement in an activity of enough worth to have endured for centuries, offering a rich history of remarkable women and men, there's all that and more. At its best, for most of us, fly angling's highest purpose is, or should be, pleasure – to mind, body and spirit.

# Chapter 2

# Your Outfit

Nothing in fishing has undergone more innovation over the past 30 years than rods. From cane to glass to graphite to boron and all, in their ways, excellent materials. With my impending senility, typically, I'm reverting back to an obsession with tradition. The aesthetics of fine cane is once again raising the specter of bankruptcy for me, but all things considered, quality graphite is unbeatable. It's light, comfortable to cast over long periods, and given reasonable care will outlast the youngest of us. I find several brands well designed and cosmetically pleasing. If there's anything to fuss about it might be that with such a variety available it can get confusing.

Since every fishing situation varies, water velocity,

depth, effective casting distance required, wind, the size and energy levels of the target species, the stature and skill of the caster, etc., the ideal length, weight and casting characteristics required of the rod are different with every outing. It's the kind of variable possibilities that keeps certain of those among fly fishermen up long after midnight, lubricating tireless minds and voices with single malt scotch. They prattle endlessly over yet one more complex theory. Not taken seriously, they are a harmless lot and if you are one of them I only ask you to look around once and awhile and not mistakenly blame the glazed eyes and nodding heads on the booze or the hour. If you are not, keep a sharp eye out for anyone brandishing a leader micrometer and bribe the lodge manager, if need be, not to make you share a room with such a person.

I think it's reasonable to fish Alaska with three rods in something close to the following sizes. The first, all-rounder would be a 9 foot, 7 weight. It's light enough for grayling and small trout yet stout enough for that 10-pounder that's always a possibility here. If all you are ever going for is silvers, chums, trophy rainbow trout or char, an 8 weight is closer to exact. The 9-foot length is my preference but I'm 6' 1", 220 pounds. However, many excellent anglers prefer shorter rods. I photographed Lee Wulff effectively casting into stiff head winds, all day long, with his preferred 7 footer. My current favorite cane rod, incidentally, is 8 feet.

For smaller streams and lakes with trout and land-locked salmon populations, a 3 to 4 weight would be a good choice. If you selected a 4 or 5 piece pack rod, it would give you something just right for the canoe trail systems, backpacking and for times when you fish south of here. Mine is a graphite, 4 piece, 4 weight, 8 footer and I love it.

King salmon and sheefish require 9 weights or better. Effective casting distances are usually long, 60 to 80 feet. The fish can exceed 40 pounds for shees with kings over 50 not uncommon and both are tough fighters, most often found in heavy, swift water. I have an old glass 10 weight I used for years, strong enough to haul a struggling bluetick out of the river but over the last few years I've gone to a 9 weight, 9 foot graphite, finding it far more pleasant to spend the day with.

Reels have come at least as far as rods with just as wide a choice. Mine are a mix of Gherkes, Marryats and CFOs with all three brands giving me several seasons now of faultless performance. But as long as you stick with well established, quality brands, size is

*Sheefish.*

what matters most. I don't care for multipliers only because they are too mechanical for me. I like things simple but others find them fun.

The key for your big reel is for it to be able to hold 200 yards of 20 pound backing along with a properly weighted line. One hundred yards of 12 pound test backing is plenty for the intermediate reel with backing on the small one only serving to fill the spool.

You can get away with only two lines for the big rig, a fast sinking tip and a faster sinking shooting head but it would be wise to talk with someone who knows the specifics of the water you'll be fishing before you go. Of course if you have booked with one of the better lodges they will have detailed instructions. If not, contact the nearest fly shop to the area and follow their advice.

Again two lines and a package of lead twist-ons will get you through nearly every situation with your mid-size rig. A weight forward floater and a 10 foot, fast sinking tip will do nearly everything. More specific suggestions from guide and fly shops should be heeded however.

A first quality floating double taper is all you need for the little rig.

Leaders for Alaska, micrometers not withstanding, should be a simple subject. You are usually fishing over good numbers of relatively naive fish, 12 foot web weights are ludicrous. Go with hand-tied 9 footers on the surface if it satisfies something within you but it is doubtful you will outfish your buddy who is using a 7 foot, pre-tapered, "I don't remember what pound test," leader.

Three pound test tippets are light enough for the small rig. Four to 6 pound test is about right for the mid-size and 12 to 15 will take care of the monsters.

Most of the time the secret for effectiveness with

salmon, trout and char is simply presenting the fly, inches off the bottom, directly in front of the fish. Weighted flies are one approach but have a tendency to drift lifelessly. Short leaders attached to sinking lines is another but I still worry about visibility of the fly line. I've seen it spook fish. Normal leader lengths with varying weights of lead wrapped 10 to 18 inches above an unweighted fly works best for me but has two problems. Some anglers' sensitivities are genuinely put upon by the use of lead and it is unpleasant to cast. The truth is I use all these methods and combinations of them from time to time and usually manage to catch fish. Being aware of them all gives you options but what really matters is getting down.

But don't let me talk you out of fishing dry anytime you feel inclined. There are times for some of us when one catch on a dry is more satisfying than a day filled with dragging fish off the bottom. I'll go into more detail in Chapter 3.

Sophistication in angler clothing has reached heady heights of late. We all have opportunity now to be as foppish on the stream as street corner punkers. It goes all the way to fashion designer vests for the ladies and coordinated angler travel bag collections. In most current mainline fishing catalogs you have to search carefully through page after page of stylish apparel to find a rod or reel. But I've enjoyed clothes since my first sailor and cowboy suits. Uniforms were a fun part of the Boy Scouts and Marine Corps and outdoor catalog sales volumes indicate I'm not alone.

Starting at the top, your Alaskan fishing hat is important and merits careful thought. I wore a typical Irish wool tweed up here for years, found it warm, comfortable and aesthetically pleasing, at first. Now it has become as common as the Greek sea captain design, worse, as often seen as the turned up brim with the leopard skin band, type. Too bad. What matters though are things like compressibility, a wide enough brim to keep water or mosquito netting off your face and some fine balance between enough individuality to be "you" and the proper degree of angling identity to mark you as "in." It may not be easy but hats are one of the cheaper items in the get up so why let women have all the fun in their hat shops? Just keep changing until you are happy.

Cotton shirts are all right. I often wear them but wool makes more sense. On those rarest of days when you find them too warm, take them off and enjoy a near miracle. It's called "I fished Alaska in a tee shirt." Not everyone has had that pleasure.

Cotton cord trousers are my preference out of the water, with wool always under my waders. In the first part of June and from September on, long johns, in addition to wool pants, are good.

Quality down vests are a light, highly compressible item that can turn a nippy afternoon comfortable but the couple of times I got mine wet persuaded me that a wool sweater, as bulky as it is, is better. Make sure it is 100 percent wool with the oil still in it. I don't go far without mine.

I have wool, fingerless gloves in my vest but don't recall ever needing them before October.

The most important aspect of your fishing vest seems that it be voluminous enough to contain at least $500 worth of flies, leaders and assorted gemcracks. I don't think the practical joke catalogs boast of more gadgets than fly fishing houses. But for a guy who still hasn't figured out all the things on his Swiss army knife and that thinks glow in the dark, cyalume is a sign from God, it's a world of wonders and marvels. Items I have no idea what they do are the ones I'm most prone to order. Do we ever outgrow sending off for the secret decoder rings?

Your vest above all, should be comfortable. When you try it on get the shop to load it down with heavy stuff. See how it feels across your back and shoulders. If it could cut or rub, anywhere, try another one. For Alaska be sure the back pocket is ample enough for your sweater, mosquito net and rain coat. And let the first item you put in a pocket be insect repellent. A headnet is less often needed than you've probably heard but it makes sense to carry one.

After the aforementioned, key things are lead twist-ons (if they don't offend you), gink, clippers, unscratched polaroids, wader patches, dry matches, a first aid kit and I like a sandwich, preferably fresh.

The best thing about waders, all waders, is taking the damn things off. The longer you've worn them the better it is. The most important thing about them is that they don't leak. Then comes comfort, style, etc. Though it freezes at the same temperature here as elsewhere, Alaska's water might average a degree or two colder, even in summer but it's not what you think.

I haven't learned to enjoy neoprene waders. To me they feel like body-size condoms plus I know well enough what I look like in leotards. I once described Mel Krieger as emulating Peter Pan in camouflage in his James Scott's but he's worn them for years now, in climes around the world and loves them.

For years I've worn latex (yes, I know what condoms are made of) with heavy wool pants and sometimes long johns, two pairs of heavy wool socks in boots large enough not to constrict my feet, and up to my butt in water for hours on end, I am never uncomfortable. Latex compresses well for travelling and patches as easily as an inner tube, if you remember to

*Silvio Masciadri (R.) travelled from Italy for silver salmon fly fishing on Silver Salmon Creek. — Joyce and Marty Sherman  photo*

bring the patch kit. Try several wader styles though before you decide but don't look for bargains. Only first quality makes sense up here.

Wading boots are another item where bargains can wreck a trip or worse. I look for the lightest, fastest drying, most compressible, thickest felt soled boot I can find. Ease of lacing can also be a factor but only after the other mentioned qualities. Make sure your boots are of ample size to give your feet room. It's not only a matter of foot fatigue but an important consideration as to your feet keeping warm. Staying dry and not slipping on rocks is vital but painfully cold feet will quickly take the fun out of anything.

I know of no reason why waders for Alaska wouldn't work anywhere else so take your time and listen to your shop people. They are usually knowledgeable, want your business over the years, and most I meet around the country are ardent anglers themselves.

Two travel bags are a good idea. One large enough to carry everything but your wading gear and tough enough to withstand projecting objects. The other, smaller, for boots, waders and anything else wet. Indestructible rod cases are a must but never mark them fragile. For some baggage handlers that's like a red flag to a bull. They can't resist the challenge.

I was introduced to float tubes a couple of summers ago. In the first half an hour I was convinced that a light, easily transported float tube is the most useful new innovation to hit up here in years. Too cold in Alaska for all day, half submerged in a lake? Not at all. I wear the same before mentioned wading gear and never get chilly. Remember, it's the same sun warming the surface here that's in California and we have more hours of it, a lot more, each day. But best of all, it's a near perfect vehicle to fish countless productive lakes that are hard to get even a canoe into. A float tube, even inflated, is easy for a float plane.

The one I'm currently using is designed for backpacking, light, compressible to nearly nothing and beats casting from most lake shores. And that brings me to my favorite way to fish.

I've been backpacking since the Cub Scouts and have never found a freer, more pleasant way to enjoy the outdoors but in the last several years the equipment improvements have been revolutionary. With minimal planning you can easily transport all you need to remain comfortable, well fed and safe for several days with a load of under 35 pounds.

The basics for me are the lightest, toughest, frameless pack I can find with the most comfortable suspension system, a sleeping bag under five pounds that will not only keep me warm but also give me enough room not to feel bound up, a tent under ten pounds, absolutely weather tight, with ample room for two adults and a large dog, and I like inflatable sleeping pads.

In addition I pack a small propane stove, a nesting set of pots, utensils and cup, a fairly elaborate first aid kit, a compass, an aluminum candle lamp with spare candles, rain gear, water proof matches, maps and a couple of books.

My fishing gear is the before mentioned pack rod, a floating line on a small CFO reel, a box of flies, gink and a few extra leaders. That's all.

I have many of my best times with this simple collection and often wonder why the vest I take everywhere else seems to require 20 pounds of "necessary" gear.

The only other thing I can think of is a camera and the little ones are getting better all the time. The

Fujica HD is one I've carried enough to highly recommend. It's submersible and takes fine pictures. I'm currently using the new Olympus Infinity, automatic everything and rain proof. It's very small, has a great light for daylight flash and fits in a shirt pocket. So far it's great.

There's no way to over-emphasize the importance of a well thought out collection of dependable equipment. If you have it the chances of your fishing adventures turning out well will be greatly increased. Try to get by without it and something will nearly always go wrong.

Read everything you can, talk to as many other anglers as possible, develop a friend or two at the local fly shops and then carefully select the best quality you can afford. Alaska isn't the danger-fraught wild place some would have you believe. You needn't fish here in fear of life or limb (Chapter 7 will say more about that) but here as elsewhere, preparation is the key to pleasant adventures.

# Chapter 3

# Patterns

Selecting flies effective for Alaska's sport species can be as simple or complex as you want. *Fly Patterns of Alaska,* The most complete work to date, for example, contains 137 color photos of flies and their dressings as well as explanations for how each should be fished. There are streamers, bucktails, steelhead and salmon flies, egg imitations, nymph and wet flies and dries. Everyone seriously interested in angling here should have a copy.

It's also true though that if a simpler approach is more your style 30 patterns or less will get you fish in nearly all of Alaska's angling situations. For most, something in between will do.

While I recall times, like once on the Brooks River,

in early June, when nothing but a size 20 Adams would catch the many grayling I could see, the other way around has been more common.

A season or two ago I was conducting an Alaskan fishing seminar at a Trout Unlimited chapter in Colorado. When the subject of patterns came up one of the members asked to share some of his findings from the previous summer. He'd spent a week in the Iliamna area, fished five different streams and had been minutely observant. Now when anyone starts identifying bugs in a foreign language, look out. What's coming is called, politely, a lengthy dissertation. Before the first *shrepto-roppotus-thermoptoris* finishes rolling forth, knowledgeable, anti-boredom folks bolt like brush jumped cotton tails. But he had us trapped.

*In Alaska you can find solitude.*

Finally, nodding heads and a din of throat clearings dictated desperate action. I interrupted with a true account of a time on the very water the bugman was dissecting, when I lucked onto the "hot" fly with my first selection. A size 14 Royal Wulff couldn't drift a dozen feet before being gobbled by either a rainbow, 16 to 20 inches, or a grayling nearly as large. But then I lost the fly, my only copy.

With no insects on the water it was only dumb luck that a like-sized Humpy worked as well. As did a Black Gnat, a Dusty Miller and a ginked Muddler, until I sagely surmised that size, not shape or color, was the obvious secret. That is until a huge, high floating Deer Hair Mouse fell from my pocket and was struck three times before bouncing out of sight around a bend.

But what is a fly after all? The simplest definition might be an insect that flies. Then, it would need be winged. In other words, neither egg, larva, pupa or nymph, it would be an adult flying insect. Therefore true "fly" fishing would be done exclusively with replicas of adult flying insects. Since these adults are available to fish, with rare exception, only on the surface, it would be dry flies only. But knowing the highest percentage, by far, of a fish's feeding takes place beneath the surface, would angling with dry flies only make much sense? There is an argument.

It's all dependent on you, what you're seeking. If it's food, fish to eat, then nets, fish traps, electronic shockers and fish markets are all more sensible. However, if it's sport, predator instinct indulgence, then the more harmless the sport the higher the satisfactions, right? And the more one tips the rules to favor the quarry? Wouldn't that make fewer, more difficult wins, all the sweeter? And how more sporting than to declare its most common habitat, everything under the water, sanctuary to the fish, the only honorable field of contest, the surface? Entice it there, meet and defeat it on this field or else concede the fish winner. You have to admit, fish populations would soar, your occasional catch, a far headier thing.

It's a purer level than I'm ready for quite yet but it's worth becomes more apparent the farther I go. And you might find its rewards surprising, enough to merit a day or two out of your own season.

There's no doubt it is usually easier to hook fish beneath the surface, here or elsewhere, so by enlarging the "fly" definition to include imitations of other insect developmental forms we increase our effectiveness manyfold.

Then comes an entire spectrum of baitfish simulators. Flies? It's legitimately debatable but streamers, muddlers, sculpins and the like at least represent living creatures that fish eat. What I'm less sure of, is all the new tinsel and flash materials. Are they much more, really, than spinners and spoons? Are they a new, sort of, soft hardware? And the most deadly of all, the single salmon egg "fly"? Steve Rayjeff jokingly calls it the salmon pupa pattern but two things about the Glo-Bug disturb me. Knowing its effectiveness, how do I resist using it, and afterwards, how do I rationalize having done so?

But it goes still farther. There's a whole world of steelhead flies, for example, attractor patterns imitating no living thing, addictively attractive to angler and fish. And my most pleasing single day's fishing in 1986 was an afternoon on a river 80 miles east of Nome when chum salmon were extremely moody. But I couldn't keep them off a Silver Rat, an Atlantic salmon pattern.

It was funny. The day before, a sparsely dressed size 8 Skunk Marty Sherman had tied for me produced jolting strikes from every stretch of holding water. But not today. The July weather was typical with low cloud patches moving quickly downriver toward the Eskimo Village of Golovin, across Norton Sound and on to the Bering Sea. Perhaps the bulk of the run had moved upriver during the night?

Paul Lincoln, a young lad from White Mountain Village was our guide, and I knew he was sharp. He'd more than proven himself two other times when I'd fished out of White Mountain Lodge. I was sure with Marty's fly I had the right pattern but by lunch there were no fish.

Chums, in my opinion, are Alaska's most under-rated sport fish. For one thing the most prolific runs occur up along the northwest corner while the bulk of the state's angling is concentrated in the southcentral portion, within a 200-mile circumference of Anchorage. Relatively few people ever get good chum fishing, but if you want to hear wild stories, talk to Ron Hyde from the Good News River or Dave Egdorf who guides around the west coast a little farther north. They've got clients who angle all over the world but come back season after season especially for these fish.

Anyway, about midafternoon, casting away, warmed by a long shot of sunshine beamed down through a cloud opening, I was dreaming of another paradise, the Grand Cascapedia River on the lovely Gaspe Peninsula in Quebec. I'd taken only one Atlantic salmon in a week's hard fishing there the year before, yet come away enchanted. I caught that marvelous 12-pounder on a Silver Rat, the first such fly I'd ever so much as held in my hand.

As the Lady Amherst Pool, where that grand event took place, reappared in my mind, it dawned on me there was another Rat in one of my fly boxes – I

*Frank Amato with chum salmon.*

thought. But which one? I reasoned that not catching anything anyway I might as well not catch anything on a treasured fly. It was in the third box I searched through. I tied it, carefully, on.

The fast sinking, 20 foot shooting head looped out 50 feet and dropped, directly across stream, into the river. The current swept it along quickly but the mend was enough for the Rat to nearly reach bottom at the swing-around point. Just over the edge of an obvious dropoff, the fly snagged, solid, on the bottom. But when the rod came up into a hard bend, the "snag" shook its head and began a wild race downstream.

Now whether a new run was moving in or the Silver Rat is undiscovered chum dynamite I can't say but after six electrifying hook-ups in eight casts I was delighted to head back to the lodge for my turn at cocktail hour.

Following are a collection of 30 patterns I feel offer variety enough to make you effective in nearly any Alaskan angling situation.

ALASKA MARY ANN. Size 4-8. We covered the history of this fly. Its name alone makes it mandatory for your assortment, but for years when we were shooting TV with time always pressing, the Mary Ann and Polar Shrimp were my bread and butter patterns. I've hooked rainbow, steelhead, all the salmon but kings, grayling and char with them and rarely found times when other flies were much more effective. They fish best an inch or two off bottom with an occasional twitch.

*Hook: Eagle Claw 1197G, size 4-8.*
*Tag: Flat silver tinsel on bronzed hooks, no tag on gold hooks.*
*Tail: Red floss.*
*Body: Ivory floss.*
*Rib: Flat silver tinsel.*
*Wing: Cream polar bear hair or bucktail.*
*Cheeks: Jungle cock.*

POLAR SHRIMP. Size 2-8. Tied with a fluorescent orange body and a white polar bear wing this fly has the colors, if not the shape, of a salmon egg and egg sac. Get it down and it will take virtually everything up here.

Hook: Mustad 36890, Partridge Code M, size 2-8.
Tail: Red hackle tips.
Hackle: Orange

Wing: White polar bear hair or bucktail.
Body: Flourescent Orange Chenille

SKUNK. Size 2-8. This is said to be the most popular steelhead pattern in the Northwest and with good reason. At times black produces strikes when nothing else will. Then the Skunk, with its black chenille body is a good choice. But it is also ribbed with silver tinsel for flash, and sports a white, polar bear wing and red tail for good measure. Drift it along the bottom and hold on.

Hook: Eagle Claw 1197G, Mustad 36890, Partridge Code M, size 2-8.
Tail: Red hackle fibers.
Body: Black chenille.

Rib: Flat silver tinsel.
Hackle: Black
Wing: White polar bear hair or bucktail.

BOSS. Size 4-8. Another basic black, its silver bead eyes add a little weight at the head making it sink well and giving it an ability to swim with a jigging action if you like. The secret is deep.

Hook: Mustad 36890, Tiemco 7999, size 4-8.
Tag: Oval silver tinsel.
Tail: Black calf tail.
Body: Black chenille, weighted.

Rib: Oval silver tinsel.
Hackle: Fluorescent orange.
Eyes: Two silver beads from bead chain.

COMET. Size 4-8. A gold tinsel body, sparse orange and yellow hackle and brass eyes make this a fast sinker. It is sometimes a good solution for faster water that is hard to get down into.

Hook: Eagle Claw 1197B,
  Partridge C52, size 4-8.
Tail: Orange calf or bucktail.

Body: Gold oval tinsel.
Hackle: Orange and yellow mixed.
Eyes: Small brass bead chain.

MUDDLER MINNOW. Size 2-8. There are a fair number of sculpin in the water here and I've always suspected that's what fish take muddlers to be. But apply some gink and fish it dry and it comes awful close to the various hopper patterns. I've never seen a grasshopper in Alaska but I've sure caught lots of fish this way. It also fishes very well just under the surface with a dry line.

Hook: Mustad 9672, size 2-8.
Tail: Turkey quill segments.
Body: Flat gold tinsel,

Wing: Turkey quill segments over
  fox squirrel tail.
Head: Spun deer hair, clipped.

BLACK MARABOU MUDDLER. Size 2-8. The addition of a generous black marabou wing turns this variation into a hot pattern when dark colors are working best.

Hook: Mustad 9672, size 2-8.
Tail: Red marabou.
Body: Silver mylar tinsel chenille,
  weighted.
Wing: Brown marabou over which

is tied black marabou.
Collar: Spun deer hair.
Head: Spun deer hair trimmed to
  shape.

SCULPIN. Size 2-8. It is doubtful to me that a fish

could discern between this fly and a like-sized Muddler, only fish can answer that, but well tied, it is an angler exciter, a more exact imitation and at least no less effective than Muddlers.

Hook: Mustad 9672, size 2-8.
Rib: Gold wire.
Body: Cream yarn over tapered underbody.
Wing: Four to six olive-dun dyed

grizzly hackles, tied down.
Collar: Deer hair dyed dark olive.
Underhead: Heavy lead wire covered with art foam.
Head: Olive-dyed hare's ear fur.

**SOCKEYE JOHN. Size 4-6.** With five species of salmon spawning from June to well into December smolts are an important food source for a good part of the year. This smolt imitator is generally attributed to John Walatka, one of the old-time guides who, though long deceased, still haunts the waters of Katmai.

Hook: Eagle Claw 1197G, size size 4-6.
Tail: Black bucktail.
Body: Flat silver tinsel.
Rib: Oval silver tinsel.

Wing: Cream polar bear hair over which is tied a black bucktail with Lady Amherst pheasant crest on each side.

**MICKEY FINN. Size 2-8.** This wonderful old fly has been the standby of northeast anglers for decades. I used it first 30 years ago in Maine. It works well on all species.

Hook: Eagle Claw 1197G, size 2-8.
Body: Flat silver tinsel.

Rib: Oval silver tinsel.
Wing: Three layers of bucktail; yellow, red, yellow.

**BITCH CREEK. Size 4-8.** All the way back to my tenth year and my discovery of the sponge body spider with rubber legs, I've known fish had trouble resisting rubber strands. They wiggle just like, excuse the expression, worms. Add this to a black and yellow body and you've really got something.

Hook: Mustad 9672, VMC 9283
   size 4-8.
Tail: Rubber hackle strands.
Body: Woven black and yellow
   chenille; with the yellow on

bottom, weighted.
Thorax: Black chenille.
Hackle: Brown.
Feelers: Rubber hackle strands.

WOOLLY WORM. Size 2-14. A real standby in its original form with black and silver predominating. It fishes as well near the bottom as others but can be deadly, drifted just below the surface.

Hook: Mustad 9672, Tiemco
   5263, size 2-14.
Tail: Red wool.
Body: Black chenille.

Rib: Silver flat tinsel.
Hackle: Grizzly hackle palmered
   over body.

TEENY NYMPH. Size 4-14. I don't know if there is some undiscernible magic to Jim Teeny's creation or it is proof that fish are less picky than fly tiers want them to be but I do know they catch fish. I've personally hooked grayling, char, all five species of salmon (sockeye when nothing else seemed to work) and sheefish on various of these flies. I photographed George Gherke setting a two-pound tippet world record for silver salmon with a small black version. I photographed Teeny with a world record sheefish, one of well over a hundred fish released in five days on the Kobuk River. There were three of us fly fishing and most of our fish (all of Teeny's) were taken on Teeny nymphs. Drift them deep with an occasional twitch.

Hook: Eagle Claw Teeny Custom
   size 4-14.
Body: Pheasant tail fibers.

Hackle: Pheasant tail fibers.
Wing: Pheasant tail fibers.

HARE'S EAR. Size 10-16. Aquatic insects may not be as prolific in Alaska as farther south and they're obviously not the reason fish here average so much larger than elsewhere but they are here and an important food source. I've found this fly will hook fish when drifted at various depths in streams and works well in lakes, near the bottom, retrieved with short jerks.

Hook: Mustad 3906, Kamasan B-170, Partridge G3A, size 10-16.
Tail: Guard hairs from hare's mask.
Body: Dubbed fur from hare's mask.
Rib: Gold wire.
Thorax: Dubbed fur including guard hairs from hare's mask.
Wingcase: Mottled turkey feather over top of thorax.

SOFT HACKLE ADAMS. Size 10-14. A favorite nymph worldwide, good in lakes or streams. Use it the same as the Hare's Ear and you'll discover its just as effective.

Hook: Mustad 3906, size 10-14.
Tail: Brown and grizzly, mixed.
Body: Dubbed muskrat fur.
Hackle: Brown partridge body feather.

GLO-BUG. Size 2-10. The deadliest of them all, especially in colors like peach, more closely akin to the color of salmon eggs once out of the fish. It is most effective when drifted in imitation of a loose egg bouncing over the bottom, freely, with the current. However, anglers who haven't developed a well-tuned feel for the take will, at times, hook fish too deeply for easy release. It is best then to cut the leader and trust those who claim fish dissolve imbedded hooks. Assuming we are all using barbless hooks, even though they are rarely found in store-bought flies or seen in photographs of flies, it is likely the fly will eventually work its way out. If you are hooking fish in the gills with Glo-Bugs you are asleep at the switch and should quit using them until you wake up.

Hook: Mustad 92553, size 2-10.
Body: Two to four strands of flame orange Glo-Bug yarn, plus one strand of champagne Glo-Bug yarn, trimmed to egg shape.

---

ROYAL WULFF. Size 6-16. Contrary to what you sometimes hear, there are a typical variety of bugs here. Mayflies, stoneflies, dragon and damselflies, big black houseflies and others, they are all here but not in the quantities found farther south. Most of the time, if you want to fish dry, you must create your own hatch but do it. Lots of times you'll be surprised. The Royal Wulff is my all around favorite because not only do fish like it, the white wing helps these half a century old eyes see it. It is usually dressed thickly enough to absorb lots of gink, floating high and long and over and over, with nothing visible on the water. I've had wonderful luck with it.

Hook: Mustad 94840, size 6-16.
Tail: White calf tail.
Body: Peacock herl with red floss center band.
Hackle: Coachman brown.
Wing: White calf tail, upright and divided.

---

ADAMS. Size 12-16. Famed worldwide, it is as universally effective here.

Hook: Mustad 94840, size 12-16.
Tail: Mixed grizzly and brown hackle barbules.
Body: Dubbed muskrat fur.
Hackle: Mixed grizzly and brown.
Wing: Grizzly hackle tips.

---

BLACK GNAT. Size 10-18. Especially useful at dusk or twilight when black is more visible.

| | |
|---|---|
| Hook: Mustad 94840, size 10-18. | Hackle: Black. |
| Tail: Red hackle fibers. | Wing: Gray mallard wing quill |
| Body: Dubbed black fur. | sections. |

DEER HAIR MOUSE. Size 2 (similar to the Mouse Rat). The fun fly, pike will come out of the reeds, raise a crocodile like wake stalking the mouse, then explode in the most heart-stopping strike imaginable. Big rainbows go berserk over it and I've watched Mel Krieger take silvers with it. Be as splashy and gurgly with your retrieve as possible and have a ball.

| | |
|---|---|
| Hook: Mustad 37187, Stinger, size 1/0. | Body: Deer body hair. |
| | Ears: Brown suede leather. |
| Thread: Heavy brown or black. | Face: Deer body hair. |
| Tail: Brown suede leather. | Whiskers: Moose mane. |

OUTRAGEOUS. Size 3/0-2. This is a tarpon style fly that gained popularity in Alaska about 1983 or 1984. The tail, wing and hackle are tied at the rear half of the hook. The front half is built up tying thread to the eye.

| | |
|---|---|
| Hook: Mustad 34007, Eagle Claw 254SS, VMC 9255, size 3/0-2. | electric blue flashabou, slightly longer than the poly yarn. |
| Tail: Two red and two pink saddle hackles extending three to four inches beyond the bend of the hook. | Hackle: Red and orange saddle hackle wound forward 4-5 turns. Include some of the fuzzy base of the feather in the hackle. |
| Wing: Tied right on top of the tail. One strand of hot pink poly yarn 3-4 the length of the tail. Medium batch of | Head: Hot orange tying thread. The head should be tied from the hook point to the eye of the hook. |

PURPLE WOOLLY BUGGER. Size 1-8. This pattern seems to have universal appeal. It works for silvers, rainbow, pike, kings, grayling and just about everything else.

Hook: Mustad 9671, Eagle Claw
63, Partridge D4A, size 1-8.
Tail: Purple marabou, length of
hook shank.
Hackle: Purple, palmered.
Body: Purple chenille.

ALASKA BUG EYES. Size 1-4. This pattern seems to be especially attractive to silver (coho) salmon.

Hook: Eagle Claw 1197, Mustad
36890, Tiemco 7999, size 1-4.
Tail and Body: Pearl mylar tubing.
Wing: Pearl fly flash, flashabou,
krystal flash or crystal hair over
hot pink fiber fur or craft fur.
Hackle: Hot pink.
Head: Pink chenille and silver
bead chain eyes.

FLASH FLY. Size 1-4. Another good silver salmon fly. Good at times for kings and large char.

Hook: Partridge CS2 SH, Eagle
Claw 1197, Mustad 7970, size
1-4.
Tail: Silver fly flash or flashabou.
Body: Silver diamond braid or
poly flash.
Wing: Silver flashabou over red
bucktail.
Hackle: Red wound ahead of the
wing.
Note: Wing and hackle color
combinations may be changed at
the tyer's whim.

GINGER BUNNY BUG. Size 1-6. A pattern that works well for rainbow and char when they are feeding on the flesh of spent salmon.

Hook: Mustad 9671, TMC
5262, VMC 9279, size 1-6.
Tail: Strip of ginger rabbit fur
still on the skin. Length of hook
shank.
Body: Strip of ginger rabbit fur
still on the skin. Wrap forward
palmer style so the fur stands
out from the hook shank.

BLACK BUNNY BUG. Size 1-6. This pattern will take nearly any fish that swims in Alaskan waters. Tie it just like the Ginger Bunny Bug except use black rabbit fur.

McBAUER'S SPECIAL. Size 2/0-6. A pattern that, each year, more firmly establishes itself as a taker of king salmon. It is usually heavily weighted and cast with a stout 10 or 12 weight rod.

*Hook: Mustad 7970 or 34007, Eagle Claw 1197, size 2/0-6.*
*Thread: Chartreuse monobond.*
*Lead: .035 or .040, 10-20 wraps.*
*Underbody: Any light colored floss, yarn or chenille to cover the lead.*
*Body: Chartreuse everglow tubing slipped over the underbody and hook shank. Flare the ends of the everglow to make a tail.*
*Wing: Chartreuse everglow over chartreuse calf or bucktail.*
*Hackle: Chartreuse saddle tied ahead of the wing and pulled back.*

PIKE RABBIT. Size 2/0-3/0. This pattern was developed specifically for northern pike; it works!

Hook: Mustad 34007, size 2/0-3/0.
Tail: Six to 8 long (4"-6") saddle hackles in combinations of red and yellow, or red and white.
Body: Dyed yellow or dyed white rabbit strips, wound on the hook shank, palmer style.
Hackle: Large, webby red saddle wound as collar.

BLUE SMOLT. Size 1-6. This pattern can be deadly when rainbow and char are feeding on young salmon as they migrate to the ocean.

*Hook: Mustad 9575, Size 1-6.*
*Thread: Black.*
*Weight: 12-20 wraps of lead wire.*
*Tail: Silver mylar tubing strands.*
*Body: Silver mylar tubing tied with flourescent orange thread.*
*Throat: Red calf tail.*
*Underwing: White bucktail.*
*Overwing: Blue bucktail.*
*Topping: Mallard flank fibers.*

BABINE SPECIAL. Size 2-8. A good coho and steelhead attractor pattern that also works well as an egg pattern for rainbow and char.

*Hook: Mustad 36890, Size 2-8.*
*Thread: Red.*
*Weight: 12-20 turns of lead wire.*
*Body: Flourescent red or orange chenille.*
*Center Hackle: Red.*
*Front Hackle: White.*

# Chapter 4

# Species

I don't want to favor one species over the other. They each have marvelous qualities but if I were only to fish one more time in my life and had the option, it would doubtless be for rainbow trout. I've found no other fish with quite the same combination of beauty, aggressiveness, dazzling jumping ability interspersed with reel-smoking runs, and as generally satisfying to catch.

## Rainbow Trout

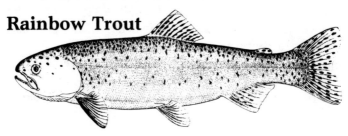

This remarkable fish once only existed along the west coast of the United States from just south of L. A. north to about the Kuskokwim drainage in Alaska. They made it on their own as far east as the Rockies but not beyond. Now, because of a richly deserved popularity with anglers, rainbows are found on every continent but Antarctica and in most countries. There is quality enough rainbow fishing in New Zealand, for example, for that country to have become a highly touted destination for an ever increasing number of international anglers. Argentina and Chile are the same. Most European countries have long since introduced them and I enjoy rainbow fishing even in Japan. But Alaska has the last large, truly wild population of these fish in existence in amazing numbers and sizes.

Maybe the least known aspect of Alaska's rainbows anymore isn't where the big ones are but where are all the average ones? With fish commonly running to 12 pounds and better in a half a dozen well-known drainages, who cares where the 12 to 20 inchers are? Me for one.

Of course having a 16 pounder on the wall is a great thing, the pursuit and catch of such a fish, worth a life-time of memories. But what about that soul healing, pristine experience on a stream with no one around, some reasonable skill and stealth required, the sensual joy of a 4 weight rod and the restoration of self confidence that comes with doing it on your own? There are at least one hundred such opportunities here, rarely seen (much less fished) environs offering all the above. But the vast majority of anglers pass over them flying to "big 'bow" lodges and camps. It's the same level of fishing available throughout the western U.S., a century ago.

With maps, information from fish and game

biologists, tackle stores and local anglers, rental vehicles and occasional bush flights, you can discover and experience what it all once was.

Fishing for these fish, as far as methods go, isn't any different from anywhere else except there are usually more fish, far more naive, than most people are used to. In the streams look for and cast to the obvious holding water like eddies behind rocks or submerged brush. Dropoffs where fish can lie just below and harvest the stream flow are good bets as are cut banks where the current slows and the water deepens. And don't pass up riffles. On lakes watch the surface constantly and listen. On breezy days it is more difficult

*Heavily spotted Alaskan trout.*

to see top water activity but you can often hear it. It will be a rare occasion when looking and listening won't let you find action but when it doesn't, break out the sinking line and fish deep.

Rainbows are good surface feeders and just because there are no insects on the water doesn't necessarily mean they won't rise. Where in other places anglers are inclined to wait for a visible hatch before going to dries here it is, more often than not, productive to just do it anyway. And since I'm rarely matching the hatch I tend to select flies I can see on the water. But make no mistake, even here in the land of plenty, there are times when rainbow trout are feeding on a particular food source and you will simulate it or go fishless. As good as it is, you still have to pay attention.

If you want a monster wait until fall, mid September into October, then head for the Iliamna/-Bristol Bay area or the Kenai River below Skilak Lake. Fish from a boat on the Kvichak, Naknek, Newhalen or Kenai, drifting with the current, bouncing dark leeches, Woolly Buggers, Black Marabous or Glo-Bugs along the bottom with an 8 weight rod, fast sink tip line, long leader and a twist-on about 12 inches above the fly. Or wade the edges of lower Talarik Creek with one of these same patterns, shorten the leader and forget the lead.

You'll be fishing in sight of others in all these places but there are still a few outfitters who have managed to keep secret holes secret like Egdorf on the west coast and the folks at Wood River Lodge. Still, Tom Alias, owner of Hunter Fisher Taxidermy, by far the state's largest service, will quickly tell you most of the big rainbows (12 to 20 pounds) come from the places I've named.

Bear in mind, myriad rumors and misinformation notwithstanding, none of these fish are steelhead.

Admittedly, they look like steelies, enjoy a similar life style and cycle but none have gone to sea. There has been a fair amount of research on the part of the fish and game folks and they are convinced there are no anadromous rainbow populations north of the Kenai Peninsula nor in the Kenai River. I have a theory as to why.

The anadromous experience, changing a life system from fresh water to salt, something that quickly kills most species, must be physiologically traumatic to say the least. Only something like a remarkably strong feeding urge, normally only satiable with the massive amounts of baitfish found at sea, could be strong enough to entice a rainbow to go through with it. But with access to huge lake systems (Iliamna, Naknek, Kenai and Skilak) where the world's largest concentrations of salmon spawn with the resultant amount of roe, salmon carcasses and smolts, when that irresistible urge takes over, there is no need to head seaward. It is only a theory but as sensible as any I've heard.

In any event there are streams, many, where rainbows do find occasion for ocean travel. There is excellent steelheading here. In fact, places like Prince of Wales Island in southeast even boast climates no more severe than British Columbia or Washington State. Ours is a fall and early spring fishery as elsewhere and, with the exception of the Situk, Anchor River and Deep Creek, lightly fished.

All you need is an 8-9 weight rod, a sinking tip or two, maybe a couple of different shooting heads, a weight forward floating line, a reel holding 200 yards of 12 pound test backing, twist-ons and a collection of flies including the first ten listed plus Teeny Nymphs, Glo-Bugs and size 8 Royal Wulffs. Some combination of the above should work with the most important trick still being getting down. Almost no one is fishing dry up here. That's what the Wulffs are for. Just for kicks, try them anyway.

# Grayling

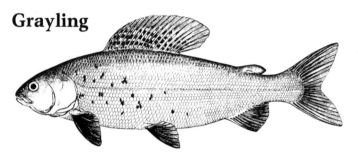

Anyone with the opportunity to spend at least a day angling for these delightful fish and who is so enamored of larger species as to pass it up, cheats themselves of a rare opportunity. The secret is lighter gear, 3-4 weight rods, matching components, and dry flies. Of course these voracious little predators feed as constantly beneath the surface as trout but I've never seen fish as greedy for dries. They will often come completely out of the water, taking the fly on the way down.

Grayling are plentiful throughout southcentral and western Alaska with good populations north of the Arctic Circle. If you find one, typically it is schooled, a hookup every cast, for half an hour or so, not unusual. There is no more beautiful fish with subtle, translucent shades of silver, blue and black and males having huge, sail-like dorsal fins. Some drainages here regularly produce trophies over four pounds.

I've occasionally met Europeans who have come to Alaska specifically for grayling. It is their species of choice at home and they are invariably pleased here. Don't let "big fish-itis" cost you spending some high quality angling time with these rare and worthwhile fish.

# Dolly Varden/Arctic Char

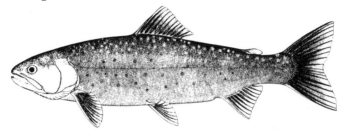

The two species are so closely related it takes a biologist in a laboratory with a microscope to tell the difference. People have a tendency to identify fish in spawning colors as char and in the more subdued tones of the rest of the year as Dollies. I think, with exceptions, most of what you encounter from Bristol Bay north are char, Dollies predominating to the south.

There was a time, if you are ready for this, when this great sportfish had a bounty on it. They thought it would increase the salmon. Unbelievable? None the less true and if there had been any real number of people here then, it could have done irreparable harm. But sanity eventually prevailed and these close cousins to brook trout (they are all char) is, in my opinion, one of the hottest fish up here.

The state record is just over 17 pounds, small by Canadian standards, but I know a couple of locales where 10 to 12 pounders are common and you can hook 3 to 6 pounders all day long. No fish is more tenacious for its size and it eagerly takes a wide assortment of flies, almost all the time, including dries. I think it is as difficult for a char to pass up a bottom bouncing Glo-Bug as for me to skip a pre-dinner Glen Fidditch. They love streamers, the flashier the better, all the steelhead and Atlantic salmon patterns work and if you can overcome one thing you will take your share on dries. The hard thing to get by is your buddy hooking up underwater on nearly every cast until you get the feel of things on the surface. And once you do he will still out catch you by two to one but that normally means you will have a dozen fish on in an hour with immeasurable satisfaction.

Bear in mind, I'm describing typical wilderness Alaskan angling. It can be considerably more challenging in waters you can drive to.

I think the closest to a perfect Dolly/char only rod would be a 6 weight, 8 to 9 feet long, graphite. A corresponding size reel, one spool loaded with a weight forward, floating line, the other with a 10 foot, fast sink tip, should do nearly everything. Use twist-ons for under, gink for the surface.

While egg imitators are irresistible, flies that flash, glitter, wiggle or any combination of the three are almost as effective. A Skunk, for example, can be

*Fly fishing the shoreline in the Wood-Tikchik area for Dolly Varden. — Marty Sherman photo*

good but tied with enough wing to shimmy and wide enough tinsel stripe to flash, it is deadly. Muddlers, sculpins and the like work well but add a strip or two of tinsel in the wing or on the body or both and they work even better. You get the picture. Flash and wiggle. Lord knows, it works on me.

I've rarely seen anything on the water larger than midges when I've fished dry for Dollies or char but I have had consistent success with patterns as large as size 8. Fourteens might be an ideal compromise between visibility and effectiveness with color a consideration as to visibility for the fish. We tend to forget that fish are looking up at dry flies, usually into the sky. Judge accordingly.

These fish are anadromous though often landlocked and the most widely distributed sport species here. Whatever you do don't pass up an opportunity to give them a try.

## King Salmon

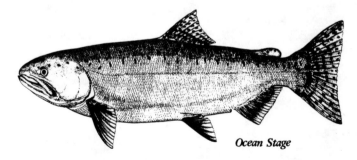

*Ocean Stage*

The largest of all the salmon, the sport-caught record (over 97 pounds) coming from the Kenai River, this really is Alaska's king of sport fish. I can't conceive of a thrill in angling more than that moment when a fish, that felt like a concrete block when you set the hook, erupts from the water at a point on the river that seems unbelievably distant. It is obvious, as it explodes in a shower of spray, this mammoth creature is well over 50 pounds. Your heart stops, your heavy duty 9 weight suddenly seems foolishly flimsy.

Kings (chinook) are available from southeast to the Bering Sea. The most northern run, of enough magnitude to attract angling, occurring in the

*Silvio Masciadri and Nick Amato with fly caught kings.*

Unalakleet River. Freshwater king fishing isn't allowed in a good deal of southeast, precluding most fly
fishing but the rest of the state offers a wide variety of
excellent opportunities.

Your gear needs to be in the 9 to 10 weight range
and, if you can't already, you need to spend enough
practice time to be able to cast 60 feet and better.
Most of the angling is in swift, fairly big rivers. Wading can be limited, holding water deep, requiring extra reach and long enough drifts for sink tips and
shooting heads to get down. I think big hooks (2 thru
6) are best but I've seen some real behemoths hooked
and landed on 10's and 12's.

Patterns vary, a lot, because these fish are aggressive, at times smacking anything that moves. But, just
like the other salmon, the addition of tinsel and other
reflective materials can change a pattern from good to
hot.

Plan your trip from late June until mid July. There is
often good fishing on either side of those times but
that will put you in the prime.

## Pink Salmon

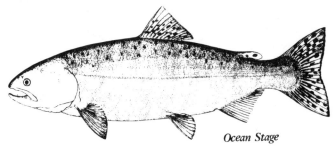

*Ocean Stage*

Pink (humpback) salmon suffer from three terrible
curses. They are the smallest of the five Pacific
salmon that spawn in Alaska, they are the most prolific and they are way too easy to catch. Oh, yeah, and

fourth, the males take on a grotesque configuration soon after entering fresh water. But it is all a matter of comparatives. If there weren't four other salmon species with big fish ranging from 10 pounds to 100, pinks would be renowned.

They come fairly early in the season, running strong in most places by July, lasting through August. They are especially aggressive to flies, fight well for their size and taken on 5 to 6 weight gear are a ball. Being held in low esteem though has resulted in few people taking time for serious pink angling. It's a mistake.

For example, there is a situation on Kodiak Island where you can rent a car, drive a highway overlooking wadable, saltwater flats and look for schools of sea fresh fish. Get into 5 to 10 pound salmon this fresh, on light rods and you will quickly discover pink snobs are full of it.

I fished them in the salt near Juneau a season or two ago from the front of a skiff and felt like I had been transported to the Bahamas. There were thousands of fish churning the water, clouds of crying gulls working overhead, and every streamer I tried, from Mickey Finns to Smolts, produced smashing strikes. I've never had faster action.

Once into fresh water they do deteriorate more quickly than other salmon but for the first couple of days not much is lost. Use the same gear recommended for char with the exception of dry flies (I'm not sure they won't work) and enjoy excellent sport.

## Sockeye

When I arrived here in the late '60s sockeyes (red salmon) wouldn't take flies, everyone said so. A few years later, when snagging was outlawed in all of

Alaska's fresh water, a miracle took place. Overnight these clever fish learned to take all sorts of flies and, happily still do. Sockeye are, by far, the state's most valuable commercial salmon with Bristol Bay, the richest salmon fishery in the world.

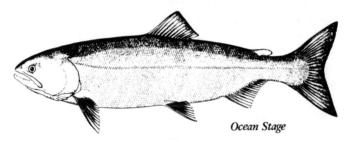

*Ocean Stage*

From July on, flying over this country (the Iliamna/-Bristol Bay drainage is an area about the size of New England), it's an amazing sight to look down at thousands, sometimes millions, of these fish in nearly every stream or river you pass over. And, given the right circumstances, they are a fly angler's dream of dreams.

Thought by most Alaskans to be the tastiest of the salmon (not me; I love them all but prefer kings), I rate them, for their size, the most energetic. You stick an 8 pound, sea bright sockeye with a 7 weight rig and you'd best dig in. Nothing up here runs faster, does more cartwheeling jumps or fights harder or longer.

The right circumstances are large numbers of fish, holding. Moving reds are beyond anyone's skills and small pods, even holding, are extremely challenging. Your fly must be down, they will seldom come up, and inches from their mouths at the swing around point. Even with everything just right though, it is still only a fraction of the fish present that will take but if you are angling to a group of 300, ten percent ain't bad. If that seems rigidly specific, at least they are fairly common circumstances. If you discover something different, please take me with you sometime.

There are great runs from southeast to just north of Bristol Bay.

I think smaller, bright colored patterns are best, flash works here too, but the Russian River debacle mostly employs large, gaudy coho flies. And I have had days when a Skunk was unbeatable. That's what makes it fun.

## Chum

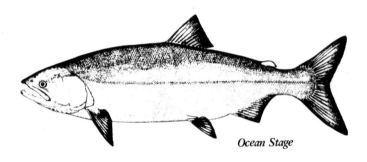

*Ocean Stage*

Unquestionably the most underrated sport fish here, chum (dog salmon) come in good numbers, the farther north the better, take flies very well and fight like crazy. Their top water antics are like sockeye with cartwheeling jumps. They can make any clicking reel scream and they are tough. Once into spawning colors they are a unique combination of silver with purple blotches, calico, and make beautiful mounts.

Eight weight gear might be appropriate as these are the second largest salmon. The record is slightly over the top silver. They show a consistent preference for small, dark patterns. And while the flash element adds effectiveness, I have always taken the most fish on black or deep purple.

If you want the best of the chum angling come in July and fish somewhere along the west coast, above Bristol Bay, to the Noatak River at Kotzebue.

*Chum.*

# Silvers

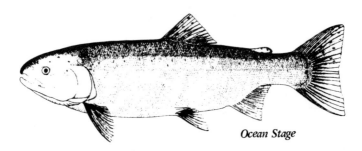

*Ocean Stage*

The favorite salmon of most fly anglers appears in southeast in July and the rest of the state in August. Since the nicest weather here is between mid August and mid September, blue skies, long sunny days, crisp evenings and changing colors, it is a delicious added icing to have silver (coho) runs too.

Salmon are all good fish in their ways but the cohos' popularity is deserved. These fish can weigh over 20 pounds, 12 might be average, take the widest possible assortment of flies, including dries and are the most aerial fighters of their kind. They range from southeast to above the Arctic Circle, are easily accessible in several places like the Kenai River and usually come in good numbers. As sport fish, they pretty much have it all.

Again, 8 weight is probably the ideal with all the get down gear to go with it but this is the one salmon most willing to rise. I have watched Krieger with Deer Hair Mice and Swisher with a Madam X, hook fish on the surface. Ron Hyde takes them with greased muddlers and I do well with size 6 Royal Wulffs. Of course you will hook more silvers with tinsel added patterns near the bottom but there is nothing like a 16 pounder grabbing off the top. Nothing beats it.

# Northern Pike

There are thousands of acres of prime northern pike water in Alaska that are never fished. More maligned than the poor pink salmon, few anglers ever try for these freshwater barracuda that can go well over 20 pounds. But then they are only the most explosive surface strikers in the state's fresh water, are found in amazing numbers and will devour anything that splashes or wiggles. It is probably the same group that told us sockeye wouldn't strike who decided pike are no good. Wrong again.

One clue to the presence of pike, you look for from the air, is water with no baby ducks. Guess why? And guess what a pike does when it sees a big Deer Hair Mouse swimming, duck-like across the surface? If you have never seen it you won't believe the explosion. Streamers, just under the water, produce strikes aggressive enough to jerk a careless angler's rod from his hand and northerns jump fairly often.

Eight or 9 weight will do nicely, a floating line, all you need and fine steel leaders. Fish beneath the surface if you like, it is effective, but those smashing, top water strikes are what pike do best.

# Sheefish

The least known sport fish in North America this silvery beauty resembles the tarpon closely enough to sometimes be called "tarpon of the north." Appearance though, is where the similarity ends. Shees don't jump with anything like the awesome energy of tarpon nor do they attain the sizes but in their own way they are marvelous.

*Joan Wulff with artic char.*

The best runs I have found are in the Kobuk and Selawik rivers with fish also in the Kuskokwim drainage. After five outings with sheefish (iconnu), a total of 18 days, I have caught them handily on flies four out of five times. The last time was for two days. I was skunked under, seemingly, identical situations at other times and I haven't yet figured it out. But the other trips proved beyond doubt that shees take flies well.

These fish can exceed 50 pounds but average more like 12 to 20. Nine weight gear would assure you were prepared if the 50 pounder came along and stream situations call for long casts. Streamer flies, especially in fluorescent colors, are all I know and I have never heard of fish taken on the surface.

If this all seems sketchy it is because there really is very little known about sheefish. Inconnu, incidentally, is Eskimo for "mystery fish."

## Cutthroat

Cutthroat are found in good numbers from Prince William Sound south to British Columbia. Though even sea-runs don't come close to rainbows for size, "cuts" are spunky, plentiful and greedy for flies. A high percentage of clear water streams and rivers in this portion of the state have these small but aggressive trout.

Three to 4 weight equipment is the ticket here with patterns no larger than 12's. "Cutts" come to the top well and lake fish roam the edges in the evenings making dries a lot of fun. Frankly, wherever I've found fish, pattern hasn't mattered much, so fish your favorites.

# Lake Trout

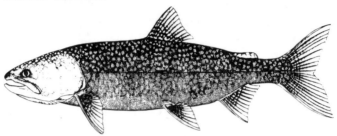

There are huge populations of lakers from the Kenai Peninsula north but little angling going on for them. While not a big draw for fly fishers they are a fine member of the char family and can be great sport.

Once while floating that portion of the Branch River which flows from Kulaklek Lake to the confluence of the other Branch we found lakers from 3 to 8 pounds all along the way. They took any streamer offered, aggressively, and fought hard but after dozens of trips on the same water they were never there again.

There are several stream mouths I know, flowing into lakes with lake trout populations, that produce very fast fishing for a short time, immediately after ice off but it is hardly predictable enough to plan a trip around. In any event there are plenty of fish for anyone interested in searching them out.

So you can see there is a wide variety of species, well distributed across the state. In most cases you will find good to amazing numbers and, often, sizes only dreamed of farther south. I always feel sorry though for those folks I meet at some of the finer lodges who will only fish for rainbows or silvers or whatever. It is like finding yourself in the middle of the world's best deli and only trying the bean salad. If you are properly geared they are all great fish.

# Chapter 5

# How To

**T**here is no question, for ultimate comfort with minimal time wasted locating fish or discovering best methods, a first class lodge is the way, but what about cost? Can anyone justify spending $2,000 to $4,000 for a week's fishing, no matter how good? There are things to consider.

For example, how important is it to you to meet and associate with angling's top professionals? Over the years I've had the pleasure of spending time with Bud Leavitt, Lee and Joan Wulff, Mel and Fanny Krieger, Valentine Atkinson, Don and Diana Roberts (Don is past editor of *Flyfishing*), Marty and Joyce Sherman (Marty is the current editor of *Flyfishing*), Silvio Calabi, editor of *Rod and Reel,* John Randolph, editor of *Fly Fisherman,* Maggie Merriman, Ernie Schwiebert, Doug Swisher, Steve Rajeff, Ted Williams and George Gherke (Gink and Gherke reels) plus a host of celebrities ranging from James McArthur (Hawaii 5/0's Dano), Hank Williams, Jr., and jazz great, Cannonball Adderly to golfer Tom Wieskopf and Bob Hope. Not to mention governors, senators, and immensely rewarding friendships with some of the country's best guides. I am not star struck, I don't think, but it has been a nice bonus on top of some of the world's best fishing. The point is though, all these folks were in attendance at one or another of the better lodges. They are rarely found backpacking to Upper Russian Lake.

Then there is the question of how much you want to see, how varied an experience are you seeking? To cover anywhere close to the amount of country or sample as many of the 10 to 12 species offered here, in the typical lodge week, would take infinitely more time and money on a do it yourself basis. The best up here is invariably remote, accessible only by small airplane (usually on floats) and far better done, professionally guided.

As to guiding, until Alaska adopts regulations, the quality will vary, a lot. But booking a quality lodge should remove that gamble. And of course, if fine food is something you value, many of the state's best facilities employ talented chefs. It's not a bad deal but with all that is currently advertised, how do you pick the right one?

I think the first important thing is to start looking early. Begin gathering information at least a year ahead of time from magazine articles, local tackle shops and fishing clubs. The shops can almost always put you in touch with someone close who has made a recent trip up here and as I travel, giving seminars at various clubs, T.U., F.F.F. or whatever, it is a rare evening when there is no one there who has fished Alaska. There is nothing better than a first hand account.

Use caution with booking agencies. While companies like Club Pacific in San Francisco, Frontiers International in Pennsylvania or The Fly Shop in Redding, California are of high reputation, thoroughly checking places out before they represent them, sadly there are others claiming great expertise that aren't always careful, resulting in ruined adventures. There are moves on here to legally regulate these services but until it happens, beware.

One safeguard, though not foolproof, is to insist on speaking with the owner or manager of whatever lodge you decide on, no matter with whom you have done the booking. Ask specific questions about the week you have booked. What is the weather likely to be, what species will be available, what about bugs, are the other guests that week fly anglers, etc.? Make sure whoever you are talking with will be on the premises during your stay and will have to look you in the eye if it turns out other than described. If you have particular needs or wishes, for example dietary or medical, make them known.

Before you give anyone a deposit there are some things you need to ask yourself. Like, how do you feel about flying around everyday in a small airplane? Personally, I love it. It affords unequalled opportunity to see the country and puts you in lots of remote places. However, it also takes a good portion of your fishing time each day. If you are nervous about small planes, there are times up here when it gets bumpy. This is a huge country and flights of an hour or longer can happen. Also, make sure your flyout lodge has alter-

nate fishing. Unless you are really all that fond of crib-
bage, a day or two, weathered in, can turn out less
than thrilling.

It may be that a facility that moves you around by
boat is more your style. There are several excellent
lodges, as well appointed as any in the state, not in-
volved with flyouts. Their fishing starts at the boat
landing, in some cases extending for 100 miles in
several directions and offers five or six species. And
there are places available to jet boats where float
planes can't go.

Every facility has its own personality, ambience,
priorities if you will. Some are better suited to casual
fishermen, not so much hard core anglers as vaca-
tioners who have chosen fishing this time. They are
fun places, usually in the midst of good fishing and

*Lee Wulff lets a salmon run.*

the best experience for the "high roller" crowd with evening bar adventures as memorable as the days on the stream.

Others are more suited to dedicated angler types, the fly tying table better attended than the bar, dinner conversations more likely addressed to rod design than to boisterous posturing. But be honest with yourself. Do you want an entire week of fish talk? Maybe you would enjoy a mix of both? In any event, try to get a feel for what a particular lodge emphasizes before you commit a lot of dough and a precious week of angling time.

All brochures look beautiful and promise an adventure in paradise. Most are produced by ad agencies, depicting the quality of the agency more accurately than any real look at the lodge. Whatever you do, don't select a place on the strength of its advertising.

There is a phenomenon I see sometimes at lodges that I have pondered over for years. A client will spend a week, the same week I have just spent, at a wonderful lodge with excellent food, caring service, good guiding and better fishing than he or she has ever known and go home unhappy. With all the above, there was still some problem, perceived or real, that ruined it all. It happens when a brochure or agent's pitch is overstated (they often are) and people believe them. As lately as last season I saw a man go home, his once in a lifetime trip ruined, because he had been told there would be a choice of white as well as red wine at dinner each night. On Wednesday they ran out of red. Thursday the plane couldn't get through the weather and there was no red wine until Friday. Though everything else turned out fine, this was enough to wreck his Alaskan fishing trip. Sound absurd? I've seen it enough to warn you. Don't destroy your own good time by expecting too much! As good as it is, it is still a fishing trip. There are more fish here, on the average, than anyplace in the world but there are still unpredictable days, late runs, high water, low water, bad weather, generators (old and new) that break down, motors that quit, supplies that don't arrive and all the other things that go on in wilderness surroundings. Be prepared and realize that when any or all of these things happen, the manager and staff are far more concerned and unhappy about it than you are.

The person who will have more to do with the success or failure of your trip than anyone else, other than you, is your guide. You will, after all, spend more time with him than anyone and if he knows his stuff your odds of catching fish will be greatly enhanced. Here are the questions. Do the guides guide or fish? I don't believe anyone does both well and the best ones I know don't try. Probably the most professional guide I've ever fished with, all around, is a guy named Randy Yeager. I've been with him several times and don't recall ever seeing a rod in his hands. How experienced are they? And is that experience in Alaska? Listen, closely, to the answers.

Assuming your guide turns out competent, what can you do to fully benefit from it? The most important thing is to listen. Ask any question that comes to mind and whatever you do, put your ego and "know it all" tendencies away. One thing I have noticed with every top pro I have watched, Wulff, Swisher, Leavitt, Williams, all of them, is an eagerness to hear what their guide has to say and, in most cases, a willingness to try what is suggested.

Some lodges carry an assortment of equipment, waders, raingear, rods, reels, etc., and some of it is first quality stuff. It's tempting not to have to hassle with your own gear while travelling but fight the feeling! Bring your own. That way you will know the waders fit, the boots aren't too tight, the rod, familiar and "just right," etc. You can take comfort knowing that if something fails, the lodge can back you up but this is your big trip, don't gamble.

I've fished all over the U.S. and in several other countries and I'm convinced many Alaskan lodges compare with the world's best. I believe if you follow the advice here in selecting one, you will enjoy one of the most memorable times in your fishing life.

Believe me, it's my profession, not my income, that occasionally gets me into classy lodges. A lot of my most precious Alaskan angling time is spent on $100 or less junkets.

Obviously, these are mostly do-it-yourself excursions and require things like backpacks, inflatable boats, canoes, flyout services, car and motor home rentals and an ability to survive your own cooking but with creative preparation there are many.

For example, did you ever hear of anyone going to Nome for fishing? It's Alaska's most famous gold rush town, more lately noted as the finish point of the remarkable Iditarod Race, but a sport fishing center? You bet.

The reason Alaska's angling has remained as good as it is, isn't that there is an inexhaustable number of fish, on the contrary, regeneration here is measurably slower than in environs farther south. Wherever it has been exposed to the public, such as streams accessible from the road system, or within easy reach of the Anchorage populaton, its quality has quickly crashed. The salvation has been that such a tiny percentage of the state is easy to get to. Thank God!

Nome hubs one of Alaska's rare road systems. Happily, it is unconnected to the statewide route, consequently offering entry to several marvelous streams with almost no one fishing them. There are three long roads from Nome, crossing miles of gorgeous tundra wilderness to get to Taylor, Teller and Council, about 300 miles altogether, crossing and paralleling some of the most idyllic streams I have ever seen.

The major expenses are your air ticket and car rental but four buddies can share that, camp at night, do their own cooking and enjoy some of the finest, nearly untouched, grayling, char and salmon fishing in North America. And if you stay out of the bars in Nome (something I don't recommend, as they are unique to the world), you can do this adventure for under a grand apiece.

Prince of Wales Island, near Ketchikan, is a like situation. Decades of logging has created a well maintained road system that can put you on 17 different rivers and streams with anadromous fish runs. Seven of them have steelhead and since the island is mostly part of Tongass National Forest, there are maintained campgrounds with easy stream access.

Car rentals are available in Klawock so with a Forest Service map and a few tips from the locals (and that always needed luck), you're on your way.

While it is true with so few roads, the streams close to them have long since been decimated there is still a way to drive to good fishing from Anchorage. For instance the Parks Highway, east of Anchorage, going all the way to Fairbanks, crosses several, hard hit streams and rivers. But if you are willing to hike along them for about 45 minutes in either direction, sometimes contending with heavy brush, you can often find angling still unspoiled. Roadsiders are rarely willing to walk far, everything beyond half a mile, usually going unfished.

Another good bet from August on is the Anchor River 16 miles this side of Homer from Anchorage. It's a beautiful stream, meandering through high stands of cottonwoods with classic stretches of riffles, cut banks and pools. Anywhere near its mouth gives you awesome views of the snowcapped Alaska Range across Cook Inlet and the farther you manage to make your way upstream, the better the Dolly fishing gets.

*Marty Sherman with a Togiak River silver. — Joyce Sherman photo*

The last time I fished there, a couple of years ago, with Hunter Fisher, the famous Alaska taxidermist now retired, he guided me to a delightful pool not ten minutes walking from the highway. Beginning with 20 yards of riffles, flowing into a long deep stretch of slow water with an even deeper cutbank at the tail, it was as fishy looking as streams get. I stood and watched the water, intently, for a few minutes. The day was sunny, not untypical for August and I was looking for that one sure sign of Dollies;flashing. I'm not sure why they do it but if these sea-run char are in a pool and you have got any light at all, just keep looking. Polaroids are a great help.

Sure enough a fish rolled its side up just enough to reflect the sun, then another. It was a sizeable pool. I tied a size 12 Muddler to a 4 pound tippet leader and cast a floating line on a 6 weight graphite rod. The Muddler bobbed along on the surface through the first drift. Nothing! The second drift carried the fly, now wet, just under the surface. When the current moved it in close to the cutbank there was a much heavier swirl than I was ready for. I choked, striking much too quickly with too much force. Great stuff!

When Hunter dragged me reluctantly off the water less than three hours later, I'd lost count of the fish released. I remember replacing three totally wrecked Muddlers and there were some fish over 20 inches but I don't recall a more remarkable afternoon's pleasure.

Nearly every bushflight service on Lake Hood, out of Anchorage, has a lake or two less than an hour away, with a tent frame cabin, propane stove and lights, bunks, boats and motors and lots of rainbow trout from 10 to 18 inches. You provide food, sleeping bags, fishing gear and the like and stay for days or a week. Shared with a pal or two this is inexpensive fishing by any standards.

The boats are fine and get you around quickly but float tubes are ideal. To begin with, they are luxuriously comfortable, almost decadent, are more pleasant to cast from and don't make a sound. You will be surprised at the water temperature until you consider how much longer the sun warms the surface each day here. And it is just enough exercise to make dinner superb with long hours, later in your sleeping bag, even better.

If you want to experience some of the fastest rainbow fishing I have ever found, a backpacking excursion, six or seven miles up the Russian Lakes Trail can provide it. The trail head is in the Russian River Campground on the Kenai Peninsula, a two to three hour drive from Anchorage. The trail is well maintained, not steep and passes through gorgeous country. The lower lake comes into view about three miles in with a breathtaking look at the surrounding mountains including one mammoth glacier.

I've had great afternoons and evenings wading around the outflow of the lower lake but the action on the stream between the lakes can be as hot as anything in Iliamna/Bristol Bay. It isn't big fish water, 12 to 18 inches for the most part but it is generally pleasant wading in spite of sometimes brushy access and there really can be a lot of trout.

Sockeye salmon move upstream from July on. You are strictly forbidden to keep any but if they are fresh they are hot and sometimes so thick you can't avoid an occasional hookup. It's bedlam. And there are enough Dollies, normally, so that you are never all that sure every grab is a rainbow. Camping spots are everywhere. It's one of my favorite trips.

Shared motor homes can not only get you to a wide variety of roadside freshwater situations but will also give access to some of the state's best salt water. And fly fishing the salt is just now being discovered. I fished from one of the lodges near Juneau recently, exploring the possibility of attracting fly anglers, and found it amazing.

Imagine miles of protected inlets and bays with thousands of schooled salmon, on their last feeding rampage before entering fresh water. They are milling under huge clouds of crying gulls, frenzied over baitfish driven to the surface. There are seals, sea otters, porpoises and whales, sometimes all visible at once and bald eagles occasionaly swooping down through the gulls for a crippled herring. On the horizon, snowcapped peaks and massive glaciers sparkle in the morning sunlight. And more times than not a large, gaudy streamer, cast under the gulls, produces a jolting strike.

If it is after mid-July, you could be hooked up with a pink, chum or silver salmon weighing anywhere from five to 25 pounds. The fish will be new nickel bright and at the most explosive, protein-charged, time of its life. Even the most blase' bonefish angler might be startled at a typical sea-fresh salmon's abilities. It's a wonderful adventure but requires a couple of special things.

The saltwater facilities and services in Alaska have little to no experience with fly fishing. Deep water trolling and bottom fishing are what they know and are equipped for so you must be selective about your guide and especially about the boat. The guide, of course, must be open to new ideas and the boat, suitable for casting. It's really a matter of careful planning and communication between you and your guide or lodge.

Float trips are a long time favorite up here and several choices are available by flying out from Anchorage. Two rivers in particular, the Alexander and the Deshka, are benevolent enough for beginners and offer pleasant campsites with good fishing but I'd strongly recommend guided trips for the rest of the many rivers, at least for your first time or two.

*Mel Krieger gently poses a Naknek rainbow.*

I know of no more intimate way to experience a wild environ than to float silently through it, seeing wildlife undisturbed by noisy motors, waking up to night sounds from unknown critters and fishing water denied to any other entry. Only canoes rival rafts but, because of the need to fly to the best water, are nearly impossible to transport here. But there is one exception.

On the Kenai Peninsula, about a three-hour drive south from Anchorage, is the Swanson River/Swan Lake Canoe Trail System. There are over 80 lakes set aside for canoeing, no motors or float planes allowed, many with superb angling for rainbows, Dollies and landlocked salmon and the longest portage, less than three-quarters of a mile. A few days or weeks can be well spent here in soul restoring solitude.

Canoes are rentable in Anchorage or at Sterling, the community closest to the system, and, again, with more than one person sharing the tab this can be very low cost.

So, as you can see, minus the air ticket, Alaska's angling can be sampled at whatever price suits your taste or finances but the biggest secret, I believe, to having your angling desires satisfied up here is thorough planning and realistic expectation. Check everything out as carefully as possible and pay about the same attention to angling advertising as you do to all the other hype we're all deluged with. If you do that, there is a better than even chance, you will go home delighted.

# Chapter 6

# Where To

**F**or describing Alaska's angling geography I'll divide it into four areas. Southeast is from the southern tip of the state, adjoining British Columbia, north to about and including Yakutat. Southcentral is generally thought of as everything north of Yakutat, all the way to the Yukon. The country above is the Far North with thousands of square miles surrounding Fairbanks being the Interior.

## Southeast

The southeast portion of the state has been angled far longer than the other areas because settlers hit there first but fly fishing in the area has never come

*King salmon subdued with a bamboo fly rod. Left, Karel Bauer. Right, Mike Limberger.*

close to the popularity of saltwater trolling and mooching. Salmon have always been the big attraction with steelhead far less sought after. Sea-run cutthroat and Dolly Varden have drawn comparatively few fly anglers and rainbow trout, though found in good numbers and sizes, haven't proved the international draw they have become in the Iliamna/Bristol region. So, for the fly angler, this remarkably beautiful, fish rich country is still, largely, undiscovered.

Prince of Wales Island, for example, is the third largest Island in the U.S. With its road system, variety of streams and access to salt water, you could spend several seasons sampling it all. Dollies, rainbows, cutthroat and salmon are in the streams with all kinds of saltwater opportunities to explore.

Ketchikan, population approximately 8,000, is a gateway to a remarkable variety of angling. Until recently, the world record sport caught king salmon, 93 pounds came from nearby. The current record steelhead, over 42 pounds, was taken in the same vicinity and not many folks have done extensive fly angling there. There are all kinds of charter captains and flight services, along with hotels and restaurants plus a chamber of commerce for information.

Wrangell, an especially beautiful town of 3,000, also has all the above as do Petersburg, Sitka and Juneau. And the most surprising thing, for places this far off the highway, there is regular jet service to them all.

If you like the lovely environs of tidal sloughs, protected bays and inlets, rain forests with gigantic trees, thousands of islands of every size and shape, crowned with spruce, and nearly unfished streams so clear you can't believe what you're not seeing, Southeast Alaska has a couple of lifetimes of adventures for you.

# Southcentral

There is no doubt that for variety of species, size and numbers of fish, in stream and river situations nearly perfect for angling with a fly, the Iliamna/-Bristol Bay drainage is the best in North America, probably the world. With five species of salmon, Arctic char and Dolly Varden, lake trout, grayling, northern pike, steelhead, and the most prolific population of wild, trophy class rainbow trout left in America, it really is angling paradise. Names like Kenai, Talachulitna, Naknek, Brooks, Kulik, Good News, Newhalen and myriad others, designate rivers that have become international legends in the fly angling community. And, nowadays, some of the finest lodges and guide services anywhere are available throughout the region.

Anchorage, the state's largest city (250,000 population), is the jumping off point for it all and could rightfully be called Alaska's hottest fishing center. About 75,000 visiting anglers enjoyed Southcentral in 1985 (last available figures) and they nearly all passed through Anchorage. Many passed quickly through, overnighting at most, unknowingly missing several unique and worthwhile things.

For example, downtown has a surprisingly good collection of fine restaurants. The Crow's Nest (top of the Captain Cook Hotel), Marx Brothers Cafe and House of Lords (Sheffield Hotel) are of high enough quality to merit an evening's dining were they in Manhattan or San Francisco. Upper mid-range places like Elevation 92, Simon and Seafort's and others are numerous with three notable Japanese restaurants, Nikko Garden (superb but a cab ride from downtown), The Shogun and The Fuji-En.

There are several clubs to choose from with a variety of entertainment. The Whale's Tail in the Captain Cook Hotel has live music and a fair number of singles. The Penthouse (sometimes called Repine's downtown office) at the top of the Sheffield Hotel is a good place for conversation with a spectacular view and the east end of Fourth Avenue contains a row of Tijuana like bars that will either amaze or disgust you.

*The view from the porch of Wood River Lodge, Agulawok River. Home to rainbow, char and grayling. — Marty Sherman photo*

There are several shops catering to fly anglers such as Mountain View Sports Center, McBauer's Fly Shop, DonKay's and Sunshine Sports. They are all a cab ride from downtown but worth the fare. There are other, very complete, outdoor sports stores, like Gary King's, R.E.I., Barney's Sport Chalet, Sports West and Alaska Mountaineering and Hiking, offering top quality camping gear, clothing and the like. B and J's, Army Navy Stores, Pay 'N Save, Long's Drugs and Carr's Payless Stores, have huge inventories of discount goods. And, overall, you will be pleased with prices. It's competitive business here and works to your advantage. A couple of days in Anchorage can be fun.

The first direction out of town for anglers, is usually south to the Kenai Peninsula. The Kenai is a huge area the size of a small state. It is the playground of Anchorage, making it a challenge to get away from the crowds, but fishing opportunities are varied with everything from rivers and huge lakes to idyllic streams and smaller alpine lakes, only available by backpacking. Even with all the use an amazing number of fish are caught here each season.

There are some key books that describe the Kenai in detail. *Fishing the Kenai,* by Dan Sisson, *How to Catch Alaska's Trophy Fish,* by Chris Batin, and get a copy of *Jim Repine's Alaska Fishing Map* from Frank Amato Publications.

Considering weather, fish runs, etc., I wouldn't suggest a trip to the Kenai until mid-June with July being better and August through September, the nicest of it all. But the world record king salmon came from there and was taken in May. The best way, for first timers, is to select a Kenai Guide service, let them know what your interests are, and take their advice.

The fabled Iliamna/Bristol Bay area is doubtless the

most written about Alaskan fishery and still lives up to its reputation. The largest rainbows in the state come from here and the Kenai River. The Naknek River, Kvichak River and Upper Talarik Creek, according to Hunter Fisher, Alaska's premier fish taxidermist for over 30 years, have most consistently produced giant rainbow trophies. But there is a lot more to this incredible territory than huge 'bows.

*Brian O'Keefe with rainbow on Brooks River.*

Iliamna Lake, Lake Clark, Naknek Lake and many of the smaller lakes have prolific lake trout populations that are rarely fished. While bottom dredging for 30 pounders isn't something that excites the average fly angler, 3 to 6 pounders, right after ice out, can often be taken in shallow water along the shoreline and around stream inflows and outflows. And any time baitfish gather near the surface lakers will feed.

How many thousands of acres of prime, rarely fished, pike water there is is hard to imagine. These aggressive, freshwater "cudas" are among the most explosive surface strikers in fishdom and can go over 20 pounds. A Deer Hair Mouse splashed across the surface can cause things to happen you wouldn't believe if you haven't tried it.

Grayling water is everywhere and char fishing can be unbelievably productive and, of course, all the great river systems, the Naknek, Kvichak, Nushagak, Mulchatna, Alagnak, etc., are all great salmon migration routes as fish by the millions return to their spawning waters each season. Iliamna/Bristol Bay deserves its acclaim.

West of there is an area of equal note, Wood River/Tikchik. So remarkable is this vast wilderness territory, the state has set aside a good portion of it as park, but its angling wonders are serviced by several lodges and outfitters.

Dillingham is the usual jumping off spot into this country and from there west it is names like Togiak, Good News, Kanektok, etc. that are quickly becoming as noted as all the rest. The same species thrive here and, frankly, it is hard to rate one of these fisheries over the other. I'm delighted at any opportunity to spend time in either.

# Far North

This is the least explored fishing in Alaska. While its attractions are many, it does carry you beyond the range of the rainbow trout. In my mind though, all things being trades, the compensations are worth it. For example, not long ago I fished for three days out of White Mountain Lodge, 80 miles east of Nome, without seeing another angler. That we released hundreds of char, grayling, pike and sea bright silver salmon didn't hurt, but doing it all in uninterrupted solitude was wondrous.

The Far North is Arctic char country supreme, the state record comes from the Wulik River, north of Kotzebue. Pike in amazing numbers and sizes are common, the biggest grayling I've ever seen were north of Nome and salmon runs are good. Then there's the sheefish, the least known sportfish in North America. It's a beautiful fish, tarpon like in appearance, can go over 50 pounds and is often very aggressive to the fly. It's not an altogether bad swap for rainbows.

The environs of the north country are as hauntingly beautiful as anywhere I've been and there are a growing number of times when I realize I have just spent the longest time recalling delightful memories from there. The Kobuk, Noatak, Wulik, Selawik, etc., are the better known waters with hundreds of rarely fished places in all directions.

# Interior

Interior Alaska, that territory encompassing Fairbanks, the lower edge of the Brooks Range and extending eastward back to the Canadian border, is not the profusely watered country of Southcentral or the sea rich coastal wonderland of Southeast. It does, however, offer some excellent fishing in many choice spots.

Bushflight services into this country are available from Fairbanks, Glen Allen, Bettles, Anchorage and others. There are lodges and guide services and I would urge you to avail yourself of these professionals wherever possible. This is very remote wilderness for the most part, more safely enjoyed with a pro.

Alaska is larger than most of the world's nations. Anyone of its regions would take at least a lifetime to thoroughly explore. So no matter where you start, there are hundreds of choices in every area. I have been extremely blessed to have been able to see as much of it as anyone I have met or heard of and I have yet to be disappointed. But, like angling anywhere else, timing is always a key factor in the success of your trip.

There are salmon runs that make it into this area and there are many marvelous grayling streams throughout the region. Lakes with excellent lake trout populations are here and pike fishing is at its very best near Fairbanks in a place called the Minto Flats.

But for what the Interior might lack in numbers of places to fish it more than makes up for with some of the world's grandest scenery. The Wrangle Mountains, stretching back across an eastern portion of Alaska all the way into Canada, are spectacular north wilderness country unsurpassed. There are long sunny days during the summer with dazzling white, snowcapped peaks visible in the distance. A fishing trip on the Gulkana River, for example, moving through this gorgeous environ can be superb. Salmon run here along with a good resident population of grayling, Dolly Varden and rainbow trout.

Not far west from there is Lake Louise, well known for its lake trout. The state record (over 40 pounds) came from nearby Clarence Lake and many streams in this territory have excellent grayling fishing.

Farther north, the lower edge of the Brooks Range is just as impressive in its own way with many lakes holding lake trout while streams and rivers contain Dolly Varden and grayling.

*Joyce Sherman brings to beach a silver on the Togiak. — Marty Sherman photo*

# Chapter 7

# When To

**A**PRIL     It all begins in April and while it can still get miserable, weatherwise, sometimes quickly and unpredictably, there is a genuine warming in the air, months of pent up longings in the angler's heart and, best of all, there are steelhead. Throughout the month and well into May, fishing for anadromous rainbow trout, those sleek, energy charged sea-run fish known as steelhead, can be anything from good to phenomenal.

Areas around Petersburg and Wrangell are highly productive with Anan, Thomas and Eagle creeks, as well as Kah Sheets being the best known waters. Sitka boasts nearby Port Banks and Eva Creek while Ketchikan offers the Karta and Naha.

*The trappers cache is a symbol of the north country. —*
*Joyce and Marty Sherman photo*

**MAY**    What makes May such a merry month in Alaska, at least for the angling crowd, is the full fledged return of everything from giant king salmon and sea-run Dolly Varden to some peak steelhead action. The weather takes a sharp turn towards mild and everyone's fishing itch becomes irrepressible.

Southeast is the unchallenged best in May and literally every destination in the Panhandle offers outstanding sport.

Farther north Prince William Sound, Resurrection Bay and Kachemak Bay will be out of the winter doldrums and by mid-month kings will be active all the way up Cook Inlet to the Kenai River.

*A Red Setter fly pattern enticed this silver. — Marty Sherman photo*

Unpredictable water levels that come with spring thaw will keep most of the state's freshwater "iffy" at best but if you can luck onto a productive river or stream, running clear and somewhere short of over- flowing, rainbow, grayling and char will doubtless cooperate. Many of the Southcentral trophy streams are closed for spawning until early June.

**JUNE**    The biggest problem in the sixth month is finding time to try everything available or even a sig- nificant part of it.

Immediately after ice out is always a hot time for rainbows, lake trout, sometimes grayling, and char. The king salmon run is peaking in Southeast and heat- ing up, fast, in Southcentral. By mid-month the wild trout area around Iliamna/Bristol Bay opens and again, if the water is anywhere near normal, it ranges from good to amazing. All you can do is try to get to as much of it as possible.

**JULY**    Fireworks are a tradition in July and it is fitting as far as Alaska's angling is concerned. This is the month when fishing everywhere in the state is exploding. From Cook Inlet north and west, this is a prime time to concentrate on king salmon. The largest fish of the season are usually caught at this time. Sock- eye, pink and chum salmon will all be available over much the same area with rainbow, grayling and char fishing holding steady.

**AUGUST**    Though most of the king salmon fish- ing in Southcentral falls off sharply at this time it is quickly replaced by the silver salmon run. For many anglers silvers are the favorite. Their high energy, aggressiveness to the fly and penchant for jumping make them a popular choice. Rainbow, grayling and char fishing has a tendency to improve. As the month goes along the other salmon runs begin to diminish leaving less and less, easy to come by roe on the stream and river bottoms. The less natural food available, of course, the more eager the fish become to try whatever looks good. It's a real advantage.

In the far north an even more pleasant phenomenon takes place. The insects decline, sharply. Where head nets were a must, insect repellent becomes all you need. It's a great time to spend some days or weeks in those remarkable environs.

**SEPTEMBER**    My favorite time and place in the whole world is anywhere fishing in Alaska in September. No Alaskan who loves the outdoors, and that's about 90 percent of us, would leave the state in September for anything less than a major catastrophe. It's a relatively dry month (most years) with long sunny days, a fall crispness in the sparkling air, invigorating beyond description. With changing colors peaking about mid-month, it would be difficult to imagine a more pleasing place to be.

Insect populations are down, rainbow, grayling and Dolly concentrations are up, they're aggressively feeding and the later one fishes during the month, the larger (on the average) these fish seem to be.

One especially favorable aspect of September angling up here is that so many folks have quit fishing and taken up the gun. It leaves some of the best and easiest to get to places, that are sometimes crowded earlier, nearly deserted and you can, on occasion, enjoy the same solitude one has to travel painfully far to discover in July or August.

**OCTOBER**    The tenth month has one special thing to offer besides shivers and cold fingers. The largest rainbow trout of the year are usually taken at this time. Famous water like Talarik Creek near Iliamna, the Kvichak River which drains Lake Iliamna and even the Kenai River as it flows out of Skilak Lake, all produce fish over 15 pounds and sometimes over 20. My personal favorite is the upper stretch of Naknek River close to its outflow from the lake. It can be incredible.

The very best time to go fishing, I've finally grown to believe, is whenever the opportunity comes around. Sure there are prime times and if you are in a position to plan your life around your fishing that's one thing, but for most folks it's go when you can. Don't be too quick to turn a trip down because the timing might be off a little. Everyone likes to catch fish, I sure do, but what really matters, is fishing, just going fishing.

# Chapter 8

# Fauna, Flora and Bugs

Nothing adds a more memorable thrill to a fishing adventure than an encounter with one of Alaska's many critters. There are moose here that can weigh 1,800 pounds, brown bears at nearly a 1,000, black bears that steal fish, sometimes before you've had a chance to release them and the usual collection of birds like jays that will brazenly take food from a camp table and bombarding terns, if you approach a nest too closely. But of all the wild inhabitants you are likely to run into, the most troublesome will probably be mosquitoes. And repellent will almost always handle the problem.

I don't want to make light of bears. They are huge, territorial, sometimes cranky and mothers are

extremely protective but compared to driving in Alaska, their danger to you is minimal. Common sense is, by far, your best precaution. Happily, bears don't find humans particularly desirable as food but people food is a different matter. Never keep food or anything that smells edible in a tent (so the bears can't get it). Hang your food in a tree, at least 20 feet off the ground, and wash your hands after cleaning fish. Don't approach bears. Crowding something that outweighs you, and can be infinitely meaner than you, is stupid. If you surprise a bear on a trail, back off the trail, slowly. Don't take your eyes off the bear and whatever you do—NEVER—run. The predator instinct is high tuned in these guys, not chasing a fleeing creature, hard to resist. When cubs come around, leave. Whatever it appears or you think, Mama's within earshot and will come on like angry lightning, if she hears or smells anything strange around her cubs. Make noise going through high grass or in any situation where one might come unexpected on a bear.

Firearms are a very bad idea for all but those rare few who are competent in their use. If you are not willing to devote the considerable time required to become and stay skilled with guns, leave them at home. Take a minute and imagine an 800 pound creature is coming toward you. You are not sure if he's seen you or what his attitude is. Scary? Now imagine the same scene, except that you've just shot the bear in the foot, or yourself. Enough said? We have a couple of hundred thousand people per season fishing all over Alaska with injurious bear encounters very rare.

After 20 years of wandering the outback up here you do tend to collect a few bear stories like the time a young lady and I were in a campground, over near the

Canadian border. It was late September. She woke up early, for whatever reason, and decided to go to the bathroom. The problem was though, when she looked out of the tent, there was a full grown grizzly just able to fit his big butt on our table, while he leisurely went through the food I'd lazily left out.

"Jim!" She tried to whisper a yell, "Jim, get up! There's a bear out there."

"Uhhh? A what? No kidding? What's he doing?"

"He's reading the paper and having a cup of coffee, you Jackass, what do you think he's doing? He's getting our food."

"Well, what do you want me to do, talk to him?" I sat up, slowly waking up.

"No, damn it! I'm scared. Make him go away."

I had a 44 magnum handgun and we'd had the good sense to put the tent about 30 feet away from the table so my solution to the problem was to lean out the front of the tent and fire the 44 in the air, twice. After all, I'd been sloven enough to leave the food out. We weren't that far from a town with a grocery store anyway. I wasn't mad at the bear.

Forty-fours are loud. They go off with an ear splitting roar. The bear's reaction? Nothing. Zero reaction. He never even looked up, just kept munching away.

"Here," I handed my true love the revolver. "You make him go away." I crawled back into the sleeping bag, glad for another hour or two to snooze before friend bruin would wander off. And the girl? I don't think we ever went anywhere again.

Moose are big, a thrill to see, and fairly common but, unless you do something totally nuts, represent no threat. Again, don't push them and avoid calves.

Unless you object to curious stares, caribou are as harmless as they are beautiful. There are places, the Alaska Peninsula in particular, where you can see herds of hundreds. I've often looked up from the water to find one or two standing a few feet away, staring at me as intently as a hypnotist.

Alaska has most of the last of the wolves left in the United States. They are one of our most precious treasures. There's still a good deal of shameful treatment perpetrated against these marvelous predators under the guise of "management", old hatreds and ignorance die slowly, but in the unlikely chance you see one, or a pack for that matter, don't be afraid. There's virtually no danger to human beings from wild wolves.

There are still a lot of eagles, though there was a time when the "managers" had a bounty on them (God, will they ever "get it?"). I can't think of anything more stirring than to fish the same water with a bald eagle.

Waterfowl are everywhere. Loons (second only to wolves, the most haunting sound in the wilderness), geese, ducks, cranes, and swans are often seen in prolific numbers. Foxes, martens, marmots, beavers, muskrats, squirrels and porcupines are among the smaller critters.

The truth about bugs is that in the far north, early in the season, mosquitoes are bad. You need a head net and gloves. But by late July their numbers fall off sharply, repellent all that is needed. There are no black flies such as one finds in Maine or eastern Canada and the rest of Alaska doesn't have any more bugs than I find anywhere else in the U.S. But remember, I grew up in the swamps and sloughs of Virginia and Florida.

Blueberries, salmon berries, currants and cranberries grow wild along with a gorgeous collection of wildflowers. In August you can see entire hillsides covered with rose red fireweed. I've come upon

delightful acres of blooming lupine in mountain
meadows and discovered open places in the forest
where the ground was covered with miniature dog-
wood. Monk's cap and star burst is common and
queen anne's lace sometimes mixes with the fireweed.
Fishing aside, Alaska is a marvel filled place of outdoor wonders, enough to have totally enchanted me
for two decades.

# Chapter 9

# The Future

In your lifetime and mine, there is always going to be some pretty good fishing in Alaska. But the matchless quality I found in the '60s has already gone down, the fall, coming ever faster. It's not the number of fish. There are still far more than the most gluttonous of us needs. The deadly malignancy is ever increasing population and the inevitable destruction attendant to it. They call it progress.

But it doesn't have to be. There are some things possible that could go a long ways toward preserving the quality of the angling experience here. Of course the most maddening frustration is to recognize that's true but, at the same time, realistically contemplate the likelihood of those things happening. Anyway, let's consider a couple of dreams.

Suppose we were able to rear a significant number of youngsters to have a deep love and sensitivity for the aesthetics of sport angling. They would grow up feeling the need for promoting and protecting the quality aspects of angling rather than being taken in by greed inspired politicians and bureaucrats in their never satiated schemes to "develop" our environment out of existence. Sound like the right direction? Let me tell you a story.

We nearly got a program going in Anchorage, a youth fishery, where we would have stocked the main stream flowing through town. Only kids below the age of fishing licenses would be allowed to fish. In order to qualify, they would have to attend a how to class and the entire thing would be catch and release. No one would fail the course but the stream would be patrolled by junior game wardens, the penalty for purposely killing fish, a temporary loss of license. What a training ground.

The mayor of Anchorage endorsed it, Fish and Game, begrudgingly, agreed to cooperate, but you know what happened? A local sportfishing club got hold of it and turned it into a mindless fish kill. Guess what the kids are learning? And do any of you think there is much likelihood of changing the hearts or minds of an adult population?

Another hope is that the sportfishing industry will grow, economically, fast enough to have a positive influence. It's coming but whether it's soon enough or not remains to be seen.

The other great hope lies with the Alaska Natives. They privately own 44,000,000 acres of some of the best sportfishing country left in the world. If, through the economic development of lodges and guide services, Native people find an environmentally and

*Kathy Repine with silver.*

culturally nondestructive, source of jobs and income, sportfishing will find a sanctuary. If not?

I have long since learned I can't dwell too much on all the likely threats Alaska's angling is faced with without becoming morose but it's important, for all who care, to think out our concerns and try to give whatever we have towards keeping ourselves and others awake to the future.

And then there was the five-year-old girl I saw at one of those ghastly trout ponds you see at "Sportsmen's Shows." You know, where adults drag children and introduce them to the joys of creature killing. This little girl was thrilled that she was doing something that was obviously giving Daddy so much pleasure. Then she caught a fish. She squealed with delight. But, in the excitement, there was something she'd missed. Once the fish was "landed" each kid was handed a "priest" to perform the obvious.

Not this little girl. She'd had her fun. No way was Daddy, the fat guy running the pond, or anyone else going to talk her into killing her fish. I've never watched a more careful release.

---

EQUIPMENT LIST FOR ALASKA FISHING

Waders or Hip Boots
Good quality rain gear
Hat
Fingerless Gloves
Long Underwear (2 Sets)
Boot Socks
Insect Repellant: Muskol, Old Time Woodsman, Space Shield
Shoo Bug Jacket (in bad insect areas)
Waterproof Match Box
2 warm shirts
2 pairs of warm pants
Warm Jacket or Sweater
Medical Prescriptions (if applicable)
Knife
Camera and film
Fishing license
Small flashlight
Duffel bag
Rod Tube. If your rod is not already in a durable, hard tube, we suggest purchasing a piece of PVC pipe at your local hardware store to carry it in.

# How to Fly Fish Alaska

FLY FISHING
Chums, Silvers, Sockeyes, Large Char, and Steelhead.

Rods: Fenwick WF 908-2, GFF908, E 90-8F
Reels: Fenwick WC4 or WC6, S.A. System II 89 or Pflueger Medalist 1495 1/2
Extra Spools
Fly Line Backing
Floating and Wet Tip Lines
Tapered Leaders 12 lb. Tippet
Dai Riki Leader Wheels .013 to .015
Raparound Lead Strips & Split Shot
Hook File
Fly Box
Scissors and Clippers
Swiss Army Knife
Polarized Fishing Glasses (Teeny)
Long Nose Pliers
Fishing Vest

---

FLY FISHING
King Salmon

Rod: Fenwick WF 9010-2
Reels: Fenwick WC 8 or S.A. System II 1011
Extra Spool
Fly Line Backing 30 lb.
Teeny 400 and Wet Tip Lines
Tapered Leaders 16 and 20 lb. tippets
Dai Riki Leader Wheels .017 and .019
Raparound Lead Strips & Split Shot
Hook File
Fly Box
Scissors and Clippers
Polarized Sunglasses (Teeny)
Long Nose Pliers
Swiss Army Knife
Fishing Vest

---

FLY FISHING
Rainbow, Char and Grayling

Rods: Fenwick WF 866-2, WF 906-2, WF 907-2, GFF 906, E85-6F, E85-7F, E 90-6F
Reels: Fenwick WC2-SA system II 67 and 78  Pflueger 1495
Extra spools
Fly Line Backing
Floating and Wet Tip Lines
Tapered Leaders  8 lb. tippet
Dai Riki Leader Wheels  .008, .009, .010, .011
Raparound lead strips and Split Shot
Strike indicators
Fly floatant
Line cleaner
Hook file
Fly box
Scissors or clippers
Polarized fishing glasses (Teeny)
Long nose pliers
Swiss Army Knife
Fishing Vest